"A number of philosophers and scientists argue that humans are nothing more than their physical bodies, yet *God on the Brain* shows why this view lacks grounding. Compelling, eloquent, and accessible, this book upholds the case for a traditional view of humans as both physical and spiritual. I highly recommend Sickler's volume to all who are interested in the intersection of neuroscience and philosophy with the Christian faith."

Sharon Dirckx, Senior Tutor, Oxford Centre for Christian Apologetics; author, *Am I Just My Brain?*

"In a world where our very humanity is called into question and redefined, Brad Sickler offers truth and hope in a well-reasoned manner. *God on the Brain* takes the Bible and religious experience seriously and views science as a partner rather than an adversary. Sickler offers a theologically reliable way forward through the dangers of materialism, naturalism, and many other '-isms' that try to steer us away from living a fully Christian life. If the church takes Sickler's work seriously, we will be extremely well prepared to love God with our entire being in a much deeper and more profound way. Highly recommended!"

J. Scott Duvall, J. C. and Mae Fuller Chair of Biblical Studies and Professor of New Testament, Ouachita Baptist University

"Brad Sickler covers a lot of ground in this short yet punchy book. He writes wonderfully and elegantly distills complex discussions. Readers coming at these questions for the first time will find his insights richly illuminating and their minds stretched in helpful ways. This book is a delight to read. You'll end up more informed, a good deal wiser, and ever more confident in the biblical story!"

Hans Madueme, Associate Professor of Theological Studies, Covenant College

"This is a really great book! Brad Sickler is able to explain complex ideas in a readable, enjoyable style. Pulling from several academic disciplines, this book is full of new, refreshing, and insightful ideas. Sickler's treatment of the relationship between science and religion is alone worth the price of the book. I highly recommend this treasure of learning."

J. P. Moreland, Distinguished Professor of Philosophy, Talbot School of Theology, Biola University

T0367173

God on the Brain

GOD

on the

BRAIN

What Cognitive Science Does (and Does Not) Tell Us
about Faith, Human Nature, and the Divine

Bradley L. Sickler

WHEATON, ILLINOIS

God on the Brain: What Cognitive Science Does (and Does Not) Tell Us about Faith, Human Nature, and the Divine

Copyright © 2020 by Bradley L. Sickler

Published by Crossway
    1300 Crescent Street
    Wheaton, Illinois 60187

All rights reserved. No part of this publication may be reproduced, stored in a retrieval system, or transmitted in any form by any means, electronic, mechanical, photocopy, recording, or otherwise, without the prior permission of the publisher, except as provided for by USA copyright law. Crossway® is a registered trademark in the United States of America.

Cover design: Micah Lanier

First printing 2020

Printed in the United States of America

Unless otherwise indicated, Scripture quotations are from the ESV® Bible (The Holy Bible, English Standard Version®), copyright © 2001 by Crossway, a publishing ministry of Good News Publishers. Used by permission. All rights reserved.

Scripture references marked NIV are taken from The Holy Bible, New International Version®, NIV®. Copyright © 1973, 1978, 1984, 2011 by Biblica, Inc.™ Used by permission. All rights reserved worldwide.

Scripture references marked NLT are from *The Holy Bible, New Living Translation*, copyright © 1996, 2004. Used by permission of Tyndale House Publishers, Inc., Wheaton, IL, 60189. All rights reserved.

All emphases in Scripture quotations have been added by the author.

Trade paperback ISBN: 978-1-4335-6443-7
epub ISBN: 978-1-4335-6446-8
PDF ISBN: 978-1-4335-6444-4
Mobipocket ISBN: 978-1-4335-6445-1

Library of Congress Cataloging-in-Publication Data

Names: Sickler, Bradley L., 1972– author.
Title: God on the brain : what cognitive science does (and does not) tell us about faith, human nature, and the divine / Bradley L. Sickler.
Description: Wheaton, Illinois : Crossway, 2020. | Includes bibliographical references and index.
Identifiers: LCCN 2019059574 (print) | LCCN 2019059575 (ebook) | ISBN 9781433564437 (trade paperback) | ISBN 9781433564444 (pdf) | ISBN 9781433564451 (mobi) | ISBN 9781433564468 (epub)
Subjects: LCSH: Mind and body—Religious aspects—Christianity. | Theological anthropology—Christianity. | Cognitive science—Moral and ethical aspects.
Classification: LCC BT741.3 .S53 2020 (print) | LCC BT741.3 (ebook) | DDC 261.5/15—dc23
LC record available at https://lccn.loc.gov/2019059574
LC ebook record available at https://lccn.loc.gov/2019059575

Crossway is a publishing ministry of Good News Publishers.

VP		30	29	28	27	26	25	24	23	22	21	20
15	14	13	12	11	10	9	8	7	6	5	4	3	2	1

To Alisha,
my loving partner in all things,
and to Abby and Ben,
my joy and the strength of my right hand

Contents

Abbreviations 11

1   The Nature of Humans 13

2   Science and Christianity (1): The Conflict Thesis 27

3   Science and Christianity (2): Strangers or Friends? 47

4   Evolutionary Explanations for Belief in God 65

5   Is Everything Just Brain States? 83

6   Doing Away with the Soul 103

7   Mind-Body Interaction and Simplicity 121

8   The Question of Freedom 141

9   Reason, Science, and Morality 161

10 Reformed Epistemology and the Naturalness of Belief 181

General Index 201

Scripture Index 207

Abbreviations

CSR	cognitive science of religion
CT	computed tomography (scan)
dlPFC	dorsolateral prefrontal cortex
EEG	electroencephalogram
fMRI	functional MRI
HADD	hyperactive agency detection device
MCI	minimally counterintuitive idea
MRI	magnetic resonance imaging
NOMA	nonoverlapping magisteria
NREM	non-rapid eye movement (sleep)
PET	positron-emission tomography (scan)
PFC	prefrontal cortex
PGO	ponto-geniculo-occipital (waves)
PSA	progress of science (argument)
RE	religious experience
REM	rapid eye movement
SESI	self-evident, sensory, or incorrigible
SPECT	single-proton emitting computed tomography
vmPFC	ventromedial prefrontal cortex

1

The Nature of Humans

While visiting a bookstore recently, I was browsing the magazine racks, looking for something to flip through while I sipped my coffee and waited for my family to finish shopping. What I saw jumped out at me, even though it was typical of the trending topics in science today. On the rack were three science magazines in a row, each advertising its lead article. All three were about the brain. *Popular Science* featured "Your New Brain: When Humans and Computers Merge." *National Geographic* showcased an essay "Your Brain—100 Things You Never Knew." *Scientific American* offered "How the Brain Reads Faces: Cracking the Neural Code."

My first reaction was "That's interesting." Then I thought: "But my *brain* doesn't read faces, or anything else, for that matter. My brain is surely involved, but it doesn't read faces— I read faces, and I am not merely my brain." My third reaction was "There sure is a lot to say about brains!"

It has been said that the nineteenth century was dominated by the science of chemistry, the twentieth century by physics, and the twenty-first will be the century of the brain. Our understanding of that three-pound lump in our skulls is growing rapidly. Our mastery of medical and imaging techniques has progressed apace, along with a growing library of experimental knowledge.

These advances are both interesting and helpful. But, as so often happens with scientific progress, a host of philosophical and theological issues have been dragged in too, often with upsetting consequences. The message from many quarters is that you are just your brain. Programs on public television, radio shows on science topics, magazine articles like those just mentioned, books upon books—all declare a decidedly reductionist, materialistic, anti-spiritual, anti-supernatural perspective that depicts humans as nothing but complicated machines. You are not made in the image of God but are a walking, talking, conscious bag of dirt. While we can all be grateful for how advances in understanding have helped alleviate suffering from a range of maladies—everything from brain tumors to some serious psychoses—there is a lot more to the conversation than just the science. There is a wide array of philosophical and theological issues as well, though they are rarely even recognized.

In this book, we will look at recent scholarship on brains to see how it provides orthodox Christian anthropology with some serious food for thought and, hopefully, develop a framework to think through what it all means. By "anthropology" here we mean *theological* and *philosophical* anthropology. Whereas "anthropology" usually refers to the social science study of past and present human societies, what we mean in this context is the nature of humanity: what it is to be human, how we got to be that way, and how that relates to God. It is the metaphysics of the human person. We will cover a wide range of topics from cognitive science, neurophysiology, evolutionary morality, and evolutionary psychology. All of these fields have in common the tendency to treat the brain as the totality of who we are and the story they tend to tell about how we got the brains we have.

How We View Human Nature

To help frame where we will be going, consider the core, traditional, biblical set of beliefs about humanity taught as central aspects of a Christian worldview. At the risk of oversimplifying a complex field, a traditional Christian anthropology holds that we possess an immaterial soul and were made to know God. It teaches that we have the moral law written on our hearts, and that ultimately we will survive the death of our bodies to face judgment for what we do with the power of choice we have. If we are made right with God by turning from sin and embracing Jesus Christ, we will—like Jesus—be raised from the dead and given eternal life in his kingdom. All of these conclusions are drawn from an indispensable concept: humanity is made by God the Creator in his own image. Image bearing is a complex notion, and there are many expositions of what it means, but regardless of the particulars, Christians have always affirmed that it includes being brought into existence intentionally by God in a way that connects our nature to his own. Those ideas—being *created intentionally in a way that connects us to God*—are central to a biblical understanding of the nature of humanity.

The trend, supposedly based in science, has been to reject this entire description on the grounds that recent discoveries in science have shown it to be false. We have no soul, they say. Belief in God is a fluke of evolution. Freedom and morality are illusions. After the death of our bodies there is simply nothing. In other words, the picture painted by many advocates of the new anthropology could not differ more sharply from the biblical perspective. But do those conclusions actually follow from the evidence, or are they superimposed as a result of materialistic, naturalistic presuppositions? And, maybe even more importantly, does it even matter?

It is worth spending a little time saying why Christian anthropology developed the way it did. Some writers have argued that the Christian view of human nature developed out of an uncritical acceptance of Greek philosophy; they say the Bible itself never

urges those beliefs on us. Still others argue that Christian anthropology emerged from ignorance as an attempt to explain humanity
by inventing a metaphysic based on the Hebrew mythology of the
Old Testament. They say Christian thinkers were trying to understand the phenomenology of human experience but were limited
by their lack of scientific insight. We will not explore those lines
much further here, because those conclusions seem completely
wrong to me. It is my view that Scripture directly affirms the traditional positions we outlined above, and that is what accounts
for their prevalence in our philosophy and theology. They are the
biblical perspective shared by the patriarchs, the prophets, the
apostles, and even Jesus Christ himself.

Let us briefly examine three of these basic elements of Christian anthropology by looking at a few relevant passages of Scripture. In the pages that follow I will explore these issues in much
greater detail, so for now we will content ourselves with a very
cursory survey.

We Have Souls

First, we will see why the doctrine of souls has been so important
in theology and how it emerges from the Bible.

Admittedly, sometimes the teaching about souls is implicit—
it is not directly asserted but seems to be implied by what the biblical authors state while directly teaching about something else. The
view that we have an immaterial, spiritual aspect to our person is
known as *dualism*, and it has been the majority view of the church
based on the teachings of Scripture. For example, when Jesus says
in Matthew 10:28, "Do not fear those who kill the body but cannot kill the soul. Rather fear him who can destroy both soul and
body in hell," Jesus is warning his audience about sin, not teaching
on metaphysical anthropology. Even so, this passage displays his
belief that each of us has a soul, the soul is distinct from the body,
and the soul survives the death of the body. A similar assumption is demonstrated during the transfiguration of Christ, when

Moses and Elijah appear and speak with Jesus (Matt. 17:3)—and moments later they are no longer present (v. 8). Regular human bodies, especially those that have been dead for centuries, do not behave like that. Clearly, their consciousness extended past the death of their bodies while their souls continued on.

At other times the teaching is more direct. Consider this passage, one of the apostle Paul's most explicit on the subject:

> For we know that if the tent that is our earthly home is destroyed, we have a building from God, a house not made with hands, eternal in the heavens. For in this tent we groan, longing to put on our heavenly dwelling, if indeed by putting it on we may not be found naked. For while we are still in this tent, we groan, being burdened—not that we would be unclothed, but that we would be further clothed, so that what is mortal may be swallowed up by life. He who has prepared us for this very thing is God, who has given us the Spirit as a guarantee.
>
> So we are always of good courage. We know that *while we are at home in the body we are away from the Lord*, for we walk by faith, not by sight. Yes, we are of good courage, and *we would rather be away from the body and at home with the Lord*. (2 Cor. 5:1–8)

As I have already acknowledged, some theologians try to argue around the evident implication of passages like this, but it seems preferable to take it as a plain indication of what Paul thought: we have a soul, it is distinct from our body, and it will survive our death. The body is the residence of something essential to the real us—our spirit. The spirit or soul is housed in the body (and, no doubt, in meaningful ways united with it), but the body is not all we are. We transcend it and will continue to endure after it dies. As James says, "The body apart from the spirit is dead" (2:26).

In theology and philosophy there are several different schools of thought about souls, but we may endorse one of the varieties of dualism without specifying which approach is best. That we are a union of body and soul has been the overwhelming conclusion of Christian thinkers through church history despite their differences over the particulars. As theologian Hans Madueme says,

> Some form of soul-body dualism was overwhelmingly the consensus of the church—Roman Catholic, Orthodox, and Protestant—either as substance dualism which casts soul and body as distinct substances (with the soul permeating every part of the body) or as hylomorphism which holds the soul as the form of the body (the soul organizes matter to be a living body).[1]

Among the things I will affirm about the soul, again in keeping with Christian tradition, are that the soul is a basic, unified, continuing, property-bearing immaterial existent with causal powers. That is, it cannot be reduced to something simpler (it is basic) but is a metaphysically fundamental entity. It continues through time (it endures). It has properties and the power to cause things to happen. In particular, its properties are *mental* properties—the stuff of minds like desires, affections, beliefs, sensations, memories, deliberations of reason, and so on. Souls are immaterial, not made of physical stuff, and they are ultimately the core of who we are. The soul continuing through time as the same substance is what provides us with personal identity in this life and beyond. Whether we use the term "soul," "spirit," or "mind," in this book I will always be referring to the same thing: the immaterial aspect of our being.

We Are Meant to Know God

The second element to introduce and offer a very brief biblical justification for is that we are made to know God—belief in God is a natural part of our nature as creatures made in his image. A more robust development of this point will come in the following

---

1. Hans Madueme, "From Sin to the Soul: A Dogmatic Argument for Dualism," in *The Christian Doctrine of Humanity*, ed. Oliver D. Crisp and Fred Sanders (Grand Rapids, MI: Zondervan, 2018), 72.

chapters, but it is important for us to get oriented to the biblical teaching that *we were made to know God*. We do not discover God in the same way we discovered electrons or the strength of the gravitational constant. We did not have to devise clever arguments like the cosmological, ontological, teleological, moral, and anthropological arguments to learn of God's reality. In fact, it may be that arguments give us entirely the wrong impression—they may entice us into thinking we can discover whether God exists just by thinking carefully. The Christian doctrine, however, emphasizes the extent to which God has gone in creating both the external world and our own internal constitution so that we would know him naturally. He has shown himself through many marvelous ways: his word, his special and miraculous actions, and his internal witness to us by his Holy Spirit. We were made to be in relationship with him, and that requires having an inclination to believe in his reality.

The account we will see later in this book from secular authors will tend to paint religious belief as an unfortunate by-product of blind evolutionary forces whose only purpose has been to promote our survival and reproduction—*not* to tell us the truth about spiritual realities. To these authors, our propensity to believe in God is not rooted in a divine design or God's intention to be in relationship with us, but is an error forced upon us by processes indifferent to the truth about ultimate reality. Where we come from, where we are going, who we are, the meaning of our existence, our place in the cosmos, the existence of a Creator—none of these are of any concern to their brand of naturalistic evolution. We have God-beliefs simply because God-beliefs have *worked*, and that is the end of the story. The Christian perspective could not be more different.

We Are Wired for Morality

A third aspect has to do with a similar question of whether we are "hardwired," namely, our belief in objective morality. We are made to live lives of a certain kind. We flourish under some conditions and flounder under others. There are facts about what we should and should not do—moral facts that are every bit as objective and universal as the laws of nature. At least, that is what Christianity teaches. Secular thinkers, especially those who reduce humanity to a bag of conscious dirt, see things very differently. The moral sense we have, they say, arose from the pressing need to survive in harsh environments. There is no objective foundation for morality, no basis in a real moral framework undergirding the universe.

The trend in modern cognitive science, as we will see, has been to explain our moral beliefs by talking about neurophysiology and evolutionary adaptations that cemented our moral beliefs for their benefit to survival. Multiple levels of explanation are at work here. Some are at the microscopic level, tying moral beliefs to brain structures. Some are at a higher level of explanation, with individual behaviors being the locus of explanation—behaviors that are adaptive and therefore get naturally selected. At an even higher level of explanation are social practices, such as group cooperation and an affinity for kin over strangers or outsiders. These explanations have in common their denial that God—the author, source, and ground of all morality and value—has endowed us with a moral sense that makes us aware of his will for how we live.

Human Nature and the Gospel

When we consider the view of personhood presented in Scripture, the question of whether we are mere brain machines or something more becomes a gospel question. In other words, the integrity of the gospel proclamation is undermined if we reject a biblical view of humanity, because, in large part, it is our nature that frames the gospel message in the first place. There are many reasons these connections matter, but four significant ones are worth reflecting on briefly.

First of all, *the gospel of Jesus Christ presents us with a call*: because we have all fallen into sin, we are unable to live the righteous life that God requires. This is a universal problem endemic to humanity. The remedy provided by God in Christ is the forgiveness of sins, secured by Jesus's sacrifice of himself on the cross—the righteous for the unrighteous. We can stand in his forgiveness and be acceptable to God by turning from sin and following Jesus in faith. This is a very cursory description of the good news proclaimed by the apostles and bequeathed to the church, but it has a key implication that traditional Christian anthropology has embraced and many secular thinkers have abandoned: there is a moral law. We cannot be in need of forgiveness unless we have transgressed the moral law; and if we are not in need of forgiveness, the gospel is emptied of its power and truth. No moral law, no sin problem; no sin problem, no gospel.

Second, the Bible makes it clear that *the death of our bodies is not the end of our story*. While the belief in life after death is by no means unique to Christianity, being found everywhere from Plato to Buddha to Shirley MacLaine, it is essential to the Christian message. Over and over again, Jesus and the apostles preached that after this life we would be raised to face judgment, and judgment would be followed by either eternal life or death. So central was this belief in life after death that the apostle Paul declared, "If our hope in Christ is only for this life, we are more to be pitied than anyone in the world" (1 Cor. 15:19 NLT). Surviving the death of our bodies is a central biblical teaching, but one rejected by nearly all secular cognitive scientists, their advocates, and the we-are-just-brains metaphysic.

Third, *the reliability of Jesus and the Scriptures is at stake*. According to the Bible, there is no salvation outside of Jesus Christ, and putting our trust in him is the only way to find redemption. However, if Jesus taught and preached a demonstrably false view of human nature, then his authority to prescribe a remedy for what is *wrong* with that nature would be hopelessly undermined. If Jesus claims to be the divine made human and to teach the very words of God himself, then his trustworthiness would evaporate if we were to discover his entire view of human nature to be radically wrong. He would be offering a cure for an imaginary disease and would lose all credibility.

The fourth consideration is about *the nature of Jesus Christ himself*. The early creeds struggled to refute heresies and articulate the complex Christology implied by Scripture. They culminated in a sophisticated affirmation in AD 451 as a result of the fourth ecumenical council, convened in Chalcedon (in modern-day Turkey). In a statement known as the Chalcedonian Definition (or Creed), the council agreed to the following:

> Therefore, following the holy fathers, we all with one accord teach men to acknowledge one and the same Son, our Lord Jesus Christ, at once complete in Godhead and complete in manhood, truly God and truly man, consisting also of a reasonable soul and body; of one substance with the Father as regards his Godhead, and at the same time of one substance with us as regards his manhood; like us in all respects, apart from sin; as regards his Godhead, begotten of the Father before the ages, but yet as regards his manhood begotten, for us men and for our salvation, of Mary the Virgin, the God-bearer; one and the same Christ, Son, Lord, Only-begotten, recognized in two natures, without confusion, without change, without division, without separation; the distinction of natures being in no way annulled by the union, but rather the characteristics of each nature being preserved and coming together to form one person and subsistence, not as parted or separated into two persons, but one and the same Son and Only-begotten God the Word, Lord Jesus Christ; even as the prophets from earliest times spoke of him, and our Lord Jesus Christ himself taught us, and the creed of the fathers has handed down to us.

Some key phrases in the definition help to show the importance of believing that humans are not just brains or even just bodies but a union of body and soul. The argument of the definition requires, first of all, that Jesus took on our nature and, second, that our nature is dualistic (yet without division).

In addition to what it says about human nature in general, the definition raises a special issue for orthodox Christology, because there must be some sense in which the incarnate Son of God—that is, Jesus of Nazareth—has continuity and identity with the Son of God as he existed in unity of substance with the Father and Holy Spirit before the incarnation. The expression "the characteristics of each nature being preserved and coming together to form one person" affirms that the Son took on a body: "The Word became flesh and dwelt among us," as Saint John put it in his Gospel (1:14). Another way to state it is this: If we are merely physical objects, then Jesus was also merely a physical object. But a merely physical object cannot have continuity and identity with a spiritual Being, as God is said to be.[2] Therefore, if we are merely physical objects, then Jesus could not be God incarnate. And if we are merely physical objects, then centuries of ecumenical, orthodox Christology based directly on Scripture are wrong. We base our view of human nature—our anthropology—on our doctrine of Christ because he is the perfect representative of humanity. As one theologian says, there is

> what may be described as a widespread consensus among theologians that Jesus Christ lies at the heart of theological anthropology.
> . . . He alone provides the proper vantage point for understanding humanity.
> . . . We can still maintain the long-standing intuition that Christology alone provides the proper ground for theological anthropology."[3]

---

2. For example, John 4:24 says, "God is spirit, and those who worship him must worship in spirit and truth."

3. Marc Cortez, "The Madness in Our Method: Christology as the Necessary Starting Point for Theological Anthropology," in *The Ashgate Research Companion to Theological Anthropology*, ed. Joshua R. Farris and Charles Taliaferro (Farnham: Ashgate, 2015), 15.

We believe that we have souls in part because orthodox Christology requires that the incarnate Son does.

In the pages ahead we will explore the contemporary alternatives to traditional Christian anthropology, mostly driven by work being done in cognitive science. I will touch on many different fields, from philosophy and theology to neurophysiology and evolutionary psychology—cognitive science itself is highly interdisciplinary and wide-ranging. Our preliminary discussion will focus on general questions about the relationship between science and Christianity and how to understand the current tensions. We will turn next to consider whether modern brain science is getting it right when it tries to describe and quantify religious experience the way it does, and we will look at some very popular but highly questionable claims from neuroscience. This is followed by a discussion of the purported evolutionary roots of religious belief and an analysis of the adequacy of the naturalist account of why we humans tend to believe in God. After that, we will look at challenges to the traditional belief in souls from those who seek to eliminate the spiritual and depict humans as merely physical beings. Then we will consider some troubling implications for human freedom, reason, morality, and even science itself if a materialist perspective is right, and see that materialism has many undesirable entailments for each of those areas. At the end of all these explorations, we will reflect again on the nature of knowledge in general and knowledge of God in particular, and see that despite all the challenges dealt with in this book, we can still confidently maintain an orthodox, biblical view of human nature and the trustworthiness of Christian belief.

My motivation for writing *God on the Brain* is beautifully expressed in this passage from a paper given by my favorite author, C. S. Lewis:

> I was taught at school, when I had done a sum, to "prove my answer". The proof or verification of my Christian answer

to the cosmic sum is this. When I accept Theology I may find difficulties, at this point or that, in harmonizing it with some particular truths which are imbedded in the mythical cosmology derived from science. But I can get in, or allow for, science as a whole. Granted that Reason is prior to matter and that the light of the primal Reason illuminates finite minds, I can understand how men should come by observation and inference, to know a lot about the universe they live in. If, on the other hand, I swallow the scientific cosmology as a whole, then not only can I not fit in Christianity, but I cannot even fit in science. If minds are wholly dependent on brains, and brains on bio-chemistry, and bio-chemistry (in the long run) on the meaningless flux of the atoms, I cannot understand how the thought of those minds should have any more significance than the sound of the wind in the trees. . . . Christian theology can fit in science, art, morality, and the sub-Christian religions. The scientific point of view cannot fit in any of these things, not even science itself. I believe in Christianity as I believe that the sun has risen, not only because I see it but because by it, I see everything else.[4]

My hope and prayer is that this perspective comes through in the rest of the book, and that what follows proves both interesting and helpful for understanding human nature.

---

4. C. S. Lewis, "They Asked for a Paper," in *Is Theology Poetry?* (London: Geoffrey Bles, 1962), 164–65.

2

Science and Christianity (1)

The Conflict Thesis

During a summer cookout at a friend's house, I pulled up a chair next to my old friend Mike. We have known each other for over thirty years now, and eventually our conversation wound its way to talking about God. Mike is an atheist, and he and I have talked about God many times over the years. A bright man with a background in technology and engineering, he was working as a computer systems analyst for a major corporation. He is always open to talking about God and curious to peer into the mind of someone with religious beliefs, which—despite our history—still seem so foreign to him. At some point in the conversation, he said what I have heard so many people say before: "I think we need to give up on the God question. The only way to really know anything is through science, and science has made belief in God pretty hard to swallow." What could I say in response to this? Was he right? Has science made God unnecessary and belief in God obsolete? Is religious belief in conflict with modern science?

It is not uncommon to hear sentiments like Mike's, from casual coffee shop conversations to sophisticated academic discussions. Even more succinctly, people have said to me, "I don't believe in God—I believe in science." Some portray science as a slowly advancing glacier, crushing everything in its path and grinding it to dust. On this account, as science has learned more and more, and the body of scientific knowledge has grown—slowly at first and at an astonishing rate in the last century or so—the old beliefs rooted in religion or intuition or something like "common sense" have been discredited. Religion, it is often asserted, was an effort to explain and account for the unknown and the mysterious. But the sphere of inexplicable things has been shrinking, thanks to the careful tools of investigation we now have at our disposal. As we exponentially increase the wealth of data we have at our fingertips, religion has been displaced, and its explanations of the world shown to be misguided.

Three Purported Conflicts

Before commenting on this characterization, let us turn to three of the most often cited examples of supposed conflict between science and religion. The facts about these conflicts are often skewed, so looking more carefully at the history of how things actually unfolded will correct a lot of misconceptions and better frame our subsequent discussions.

Copernicus, Galileo, and Heliocentrism

In the history of the relationship between science and religion, one event towers over all others as an example of the deep-seated tension sometimes seen to exist. The conflict between the Catholic Church and astronomers over heliocentrism is often portrayed as an argument between scientists, interested only in the truth of the matter, and the church, which was indifferent to the facts because of its dogmatism. But that does not capture all the nuances involved and, in some important ways, is even inaccurate. In reality, many different elements contributed to the eventual clash between the Catholic Church and the new cosmology. The disputes are more subtle and interesting than they are often presented to be.

At issue was the question of which body orbited which: did the earth orbit the sun, or did the sun orbit the earth? Throughout the Middle Ages, astronomy was based on a cosmological model very common in the ancient world. In this picture of the cosmos, the earth was at the center, and the sun, moon, planets, and stars all re-volved around the earth. This model was articulated convincingly by Aristotle in fourth-century-BC classical Greece, and later pre-sented in sophisticated detail by Ptolemy in Roman Egypt during the second century AD. Their work provided the framework for astronomy that lasted throughout the medieval period. Problems emerged for the church, however, because it also claimed justifica-tion for geocentrism in Christian Scripture, citing Psalm 102:25:

> Of old you laid the foundation of the earth,
>   and the heavens are the work of your hands.

The example of Joshua ordering the sun to stand still seemed to provide another argument for geocentrism (Josh. 10). The biblical account clearly states that it was the *sun* that stood still while the Israelites fought; but the implication from that must be that the sun is normally moving and was prevented from moving only by a miracle.

But it was more than allegiance to a literal interpretation of the Bible that led the church and Galileo into conflict. In addition to apparent biblical teaching, many commonsense arguments fa-vored geocentrism. Our everyday observations plausibly indicate that we are stable and unmoving. When an object is dropped, for example, it moves down in a straight line, not curving backward as if the earth is rotating underneath it. There is also variation in the strength and direction of the wind, but if we were hurtling through space, we might expect a constant headwind, always from the same direction, as we plow forward. These and similar arguments underscore the powerful feeling that we have: the earth is stationary. But those commonsense prejudices, apparently reinforced by the Bible, were soon to clash with the evidence—not in a dramatic defeat resulting from a sudden onslaught of proofs, but rather in a long, protracted war of attrition.

In 1543, Copernicus's *On the Revolutions of the Celestial Spheres*, in which he laid out his model of heliocentrism, was published just before his death. He had been working on the observations that led to the publication for thirty years, and it was only after considerable prompting that he published those findings at all (interestingly enough, in a work dedicated to the pope). In his mind, the work was still incomplete and inconclusive. Contrary to the way it is often depicted, there was no clearly compelling case made in *Revolutions* sufficient for toppling the geocentric model favored by the church. Essentially no new empirical, observational evidence appeared in his publication. His purpose was to alter the model, not trot out an army of data.

When Copernicus developed his heliocentric model, it fared no better at fitting the data than did the older geocentrism based on Ptolemy. Thus, the early debate was not between a system that fit the data (Copernicus's) and one that did not (Ptolemy's), as it is so often rendered. Instead, the two systems were roughly equal in terms of according with observations.

Not until the early 1600s was another gifted astronomer, the Italian Galileo Galilei, able to demonstrate that the sun-centered system was not just another model; its truth could be shown by observation. Aided by a newly invented means of magnification, the telescope, Galileo chronicled several observable features of our solar system that were in conflict with the claims of Aristotle and Ptolemy. For example, he observed that Jupiter had four moons in its orbit, that Venus also had phases like the earth's moon, and that the surface of the moon was not smooth, as had been claimed by Aristotle, but full of peaks and valleys. Richard J. Blackwell points out:

As the generations passed, some new evidence slowly accumulated that tended to make the new cosmic theory more likely to be true. In Galileo's day, however, conclusive proof of Copernicanism still had not been found, despite his own lifelong efforts to establish such a proof. To understand the Galileo affair properly, it is essential to keep in mind that no one, including Galileo himself, was yet able to settle the scientific debate conclusively.[1]

Note the qualifiers used in Blackwell's description: evidence "slowly accumulated" that "tended" to make the new theory "more likely." That hardly fits the depiction of overwhelming proof being rejected out of religious prejudice that accounts of these events often give. The Galilean controversy cannot be properly understood as long as it is treated simply as a question of science versus religion. In fact, there was another important alternative, one that tried to combine both geocentrism and a modified heliocentrism. The late sixteenth-century work of Danish astronomer Tycho Brahe attempted to do just that by making the earth the center of the solar system and having the sun orbit around it, but making the sun the center of the other planets' orbits while it traveled around the earth. Thus did Brahe try to combine features of both models to fit the observations and attain other goals for the cosmological models. Galileo's observations were consistent with Brahe's model as well as with Copernicus's, even if they were inconsistent with Aristotelian science and Ptolemaism. Theory choice was not to be decided then by simply taking note of the data and letting it compel one single, clearly preferable conclusion.

In addition, some scholars have argued that there was strong reason to resist the abrupt paradigm change offered by heliocentrism that went beyond the astronomical data itself. Aristotelian natural philosophy, which served as the broad framework for the geocentric model endorsed by medieval philosophers and church

---

1. Richard J. Blackwell, "Galileo Galilei," in *Science and Religion: A Historical Introduction*, ed. Gary B. Ferngren (Baltimore: Johns Hopkins University Press, 2002), 109.

officials, had been remarkably successful at providing scientific insight and explanation. Though geocentrism and heliocentrism rated about the same when it came to fitting astronomical data, there were other theoretical points to consider. For example, Aristotle's theories of natural place and natural motion, crucial components of the Ptolemaic system, are inconsistent with heliocentrism. It was clear to the astronomers and theologians of the period that accepting heliocentrism meant throwing out the best, most successful scientific theories of the day. This was a high price to pay for a model that offered no compelling empirical advantages. As historian of science David Lindberg summarizes, "The Aristotelian corpus offered a convincing framework and a powerful methodology for thinking and writing about cosmology, meteorology, psychology, matter theory, motion, light, sensation, and biological phenomena of all kinds—Aristotelian philosophy was simply too valuable to relinquish."[2] A contemporary parallel would be rejecting atomic theory, which serves as the foundation of nearly every modern branch of science.

To be sure, political and theological forces took over later in Galileo's career, even forcing him to recant his teachings and spend his waning years under house arrest. That Italy's finest scientist of the age was subjected to such bullying is surely tragic, but should not be cast as a conflict between science and religion per se. After all, Galileo also called himself a Christian, claimed to believe in the authority of the Bible, and was theologically informed and wont to make theological arguments. Furthermore, even among astronomers and cosmologists, heliocentrism remained a minority opinion in his day. As Lindberg says, "It follows that the conflict was located as much *within* the church (between opposing theories of biblical interpretation) and *within* science (between alternative cosmologies) as *between* science and the church."[3]

---

2. David Lindberg, "Medieval Science and Religion," in Ferngren, *Science and Religion*, 67.

3. Lindberg, "Medieval Science and Religion," 58.

Newton and Mechanism

In the seventeenth century, the brilliant work of Sir Isaac Newton highlighted and sharpened another issue that would strain the relationship between science and religion over the next few centuries. There were already some stirrings as scientists (then called "natural philosophers") began developing mechanical models of matter, according to which all visible objects are composed of matter in motion, and all observable qualities of those objects can be reduced to and explained by those motions. But, again, the question arose, what are the implications of these views for theology? Are the new findings compatible with traditional Christianity? Conflicts and difficulties began to arise with the work of Thomas Hobbes, Pierre Gassendi, René Descartes, Robert Boyle, Francis Bacon, and others pursuing mechanical models. John Locke, for example, was accused of undermining the doctrine of original sin with his "environmental" view of the mind as a *tabula rasa* (or "blank slate") to which nothing but experience could contribute content. Descartes struggled to explain how the Catholic doctrine of transubstantiation, which says that the elements of Communion become the body and blood of Christ, could be harmonized with the view that matter in motion is solely responsible for a thing's properties. Gassendi tried to understand how human free will could be preserved if all of one's actions result from laws of motion operating on matter, which would apparently determine our bodies' actions for us and do away with freedom. Boyle expressed concern about the atheism still associated with Epicureanism, the intellectual ancestor of his own corpuscular theory. In this environment, Newton began his work, accepting the mechanical philosophy as a student at Cambridge, and also paying attention to theological concerns.[4]

---

4. For an excellent discussion of the theological concerns of the mechanical philosophers, see Margaret J. Osler, *Divine Will and the Mechanical Philosophy: Gassendi and Descartes on Contingency and Necessity in the Created World* (New York: Cambridge University Press, 2004).

Newton was able to model the behavior of celestial bodies (including the earth, moon, and sun) through mechanical means by positing that one force, the force of gravity, was responsible for terrestrial phenomena, such as the falling of heavy bodies to earth, as well as celestial phenomena, such as the earth's orbit around the sun. His insight here was in noting that the same force that caused apples to fall to the earth (terrestrial events) caused the moon and planets to stay in their orbits (celestial events). Through his clever combination of observation and mathematical modeling, he also formulated his three famous laws of motion: (1) that a body at rest will stay at rest, and a body at motion will continue in uniform motion, unless acted on by an external force; (2) that a force of strength F applied to a body of mass m results in an acceleration of a; and (3) that every action is paired with an equal and opposite reaction.

The result of this comprehensive and powerful work was the ability to account for nearly all natural phenomena from a few carefully stated physical principles. Even though Newton frequently referred to the activity of God in nature (for example, that God might be directly responsible for gravitational attraction in the absence of a materially mediated force, or that the smallest particles of matter were made to be indestructible by God so that nature would behave uniformly through time), later thinkers such as French scientist Pierre-Simon Laplace (sometimes called "the French Newton") noted that there was nothing in Newton's system of nature that required God, or any intelligent agent at all. The properties of matter in motion seemed sufficient to explain the behavior of natural objects. Newton's was an apparently complete system amenable to a fully naturalistic interpretation.

Interestingly, people drew two diametrically opposed inferences from Newton's work. On the one hand, many people saw the success of Newton (and many people see the continued success of physics to the present day) as pushing God to the sidelines and threatening the traditional doctrine that God is sovereign and actively holding the universe together. If God is not needed to explain the behavior of the world because natural laws are sufficient, and if the cosmos, like a giant clock, operates on mechanical principles alone, then one has no reason to suppose that God even exists except as a distant deistic Creator—someone who wound up the clock and has not been involved since. There would be no explanatory role for God to play. Newton himself rejected this interpretation. He considered God to have a vital role in setting up the initial conditions for the universe, but also in providing the means for its continued stability. Not all of Newton's followers agreed. As historian of science James Turner observes:

> A willful personal God jarred many sensibilities in the eighteenth century. . . . The mechanistic strain in seventeenth century science suggested instead a more impersonal Deity ruling through invariable natural laws. . . . Newton the mechanist suppressed in public consciousness the complexities of the real Newton. The great philosopher's excursions into esoteric realms of alchemy and prophecy were forgotten by a people who found it embarrassing to recall that their scientific hero had believed physical appearances only a veil over a deeper spiritual reality. Science inclined increasingly toward God the Watchmaker [who] did not have to wind His watch at all.[5]

Newton, on the other hand, saw his work in physics as clearly providing evidence of God's design and providence. Others also saw the success of Newton's work, and the picture that eventually developed of the universe as a giant machine (a picture Newton did not endorse[6]), as a strong argument for theism.

---

5. James Turner, *Without God, without Creed: The Origins of Unbelief in America* (Baltimore: Johns Hopkins University Press, 1986), 35–36.

6. There is a question of the degree to which Newton was a "Newtonian" in this sense. See Edward Davis, "Newton's Rejection of the 'Newtonian Worldview': The Role of Divine Will in Newton's Natural Philosophy," in *Facets of Faith and Science*, vol. 3, *The Role of Beliefs in the Natural Sciences*, ed. Jitse M. van der Meer (Lanham, MD: University Press of America, 1996), 75–96.

It was just this image of the cosmos as a well-constructed machine that prompted William Paley, eighteenth-century English clergyman and apologist, to give his famous watch analogy. Paley argued that one would not suppose that a fine watch found in the forest was the result of chance but would infer that there must have been a watchmaker. In the same way, Paley said that the existence of a finely crafted universe compels us to believe that the universe must have been designed as well. For Paley, the complexity of the world spoke in favor of God's existence, not against it. The world could have been chaotic, but it is not: it is lawlike, consistent in its behavior, and well adjusted to support the needs of life. But to many scientists, the role for God in explaining the workings of the universe had clearly been put in jeopardy, and referring to God's activity as an explanatory stopgap was increasingly seen as indolent. Even those who believed in God's action in the universe were increasingly likely to describe God as working indirectly in the world through secondary causes, rather than directly as a primary cause.

Darwin and Evolution

The most noted recent battle between science and religion developed over the theories of Charles Darwin. Darwin proposed a theory of the development of species that depended not on God but merely on natural processes operating according to natural laws. The elegance of the theory was that it offered an account that, if accurate, would explain how the wide array of life forms we see today could have developed from much simpler forms of life in the ancient past. Most notably, it would do so naturalistically—that is, without reference to divine creation or divine intervention in nature. Prior to Darwin's work, teleological (or "design") arguments were standard fare in arguing for the existence of God: surely life, being as complex as it is, was designed and therefore requires a designer. But by accounting for the elegance and variation of living beings without God, in the words of modern zoologist Richard Dawkins, "Darwin made it possible to be an intellectually fulfilled atheist."[7]

According to the late nineteenth-century accounts of evolution by Andrew Dickson White and John William Draper, Darwin's writings sparked another in an ongoing series of battles between science and religion. The opening chapters of the biblical book of Genesis depict creation as taking place at the direct behest of God in just a few days, and humans in particular were described as the pinnacle of God's creation, formed directly by God from the dust of the earth. The theory of evolution painted a very different picture, with long eons of time stretching back millions of years, where humans simply mark another point of development along the way. Death would not have entered paradise following the sin of Adam, as the biblical narrative describes it, but would have preceded any humans by hundreds of millions of years.

Like the debates over heliocentrism and mechanism, however, the debate over evolution has a more complicated history than the standard Draper and White warfare model describes. The initial reception of Darwin's theory, for example, was mixed: many biologists opposed it on scientific grounds, and many Christians supported it largely on theological grounds. Darwin himself, for one, seemed to think *On the Origins of Species* to be quite friendly to theism. Philosopher Charles Taliaferro explains:

> There was some reason to read Darwin's work as compatible with theistic faith. After all, Darwin himself contended that the laws he identified show us God's mode of creation. There is even an attenuated utilitarian theodicy at play in his biology. . . . The word "creation" is used widely throughout *Origins of Species*, more than a hundred times. The book also begins with a passage from Francis Bacon extolling the study of God's works, along with another theistic passage. Some prominent Anglicans and others welcomed Darwin's work as revealing God's

---

7. Richard Dawkins, *The Blind Watchmaker* (New York: Norton, 1986), 6.

broader, ongoing creative work [such as] Charles Kingsley, Aubrey Moore, and Frederick Temple, Archbishop of Canterbury.[8]

That is not to say that Christians were generally receptive but to point out that the response was wide-ranging. In fact, the reaction to Darwin over the ensuing decades was so variegated that generalizations about the reception he received in the religious community are likely to lapse into caricature. As historian David Livingstone comments:

> The sweep of opinion [could be] repeated many times over. Francis Orpen Morris, for example, an Anglican rector in Yorkshire, thought Darwinism deserved only "ineffable contempt and indignation." The American Baptist theologian A. H. Strong, by contrast, insisted that "the attraction of gravitation and the principle of evolution are only other names for Christ." The Scottish cleric William Miller felt that humanity's ultimate choice was—to use the title of his 1900 volume—*God . . . or Natural Selection?* His evangelical fellow countryman Henry Drummond, on the other hand, tried vigorously in *Natural Law in the Spiritual World* (1883) to Darwinize theology and to import evolutionary laws into the supernatural realm.[9]

Yet, despite the swaggering confidence of people like Dawkins, many people remain skeptical of naturalistic evolution. For over three decades Gallup has been conducting a poll on Americans' beliefs about origins, and the findings have been remarkably stable. Over two hundred years after Darwin's birth in 1809, around 45 percent of Americans believe that humans were created directly by God in their present form—the same number that believed the same claim in 1982 when Gallup initiated the poll. Over 30 percent believe that evolution has taken place but that it was di-

---

8. Charles Taliaferro, *Evidence and Faith: Philosophy and Religion since the Seventeenth Century* (New York: Cambridge University Press, 2005), 258.

9. David N. Livingstone, "Re-Placing Darwinism and Christianity," in *When Science and Christianity Meet*, ed. David C. Lindberg and Ronald L. Numbers (Chicago: University of Chicago Press, 2003), 197.

rected by God. When these conclusions are combined, we see that nearly 80 percent believe that God created life either directly or through evolution, and only around 15 percent believe that "humans evolved, but that God had no part in the process."[10] Clearly the issue of origins and God's role in creation (if any) is still very much alive today, and many scientists and religious people believe that religion and evolution can coexist.

Has Science Displaced Christianity?

The issues are complicated, as we have seen. So, what have scientists supposedly learned that makes religious claims doubtful or brings them under a cloud of suspicion? Primarily it is the view that science has displaced religion by answering questions through natural explanations, whereas religious people answer those same questions by invoking God out of ignorance. On this account, God (or the gods) was the explanation for thunder and lightning; now we know they are not divine wrath but the product of moving pressure systems and the dramatic discharge of a built-up surplus of electrons. Earthquakes and volcanoes, floods and droughts, plagues and pestilence—these are not the caprice of deities but the result of wholly natural and discoverable processes. Their results are tragic but not without scientific explanation. The tendency to fill in explanations with God when nothing natural is available is known as "god-of-the-gaps" thinking, and it is the subject of much derision from skeptics.

Dawkins, a famed Oxford atheist and science writer, claims to find examples of this reasoning especially prevalent among young-earth creationists and Intelligent Design advocates, both of whom he confusingly calls "creationists."[11] They are his favorite

10. "Evolution, Creationism, Intelligent Design," Gallup, accessed August 4, 2017, http://www.gallup.com/poll/21814/evolution-creationism-intelligent-design.aspx.
11. Anyone who believes that God is the Creator is a creationist, but Dawkins has in mind the young-earth view that the world and cosmos were made somewhere around six thousand years ago, and the Intelligent Design view that certain features of the natural world defy a purely naturalistic explanation even if evolution is a part of the account.

targets for leveling his accusation of using god-of-the-gaps arguments. Dawkins says: "Creationists eagerly seek a gap in present day knowledge or understanding. If an apparent gap is found, it is *assumed* that God, by default, must fill it. [But] gaps shrink as science advances, and God is threatened with eventually having nothing to do and nowhere to hide."[12] He also says: "Gaps, by default in the mind of the creationist, are filled by God. Areas where there is a lack of data, or a lack of understanding, are automatically assumed to belong, by default, to God."[13] It is as if, Dawkins says, we were to witness a magic trick that we could not explain or understand, and then—based on our own incredulity and mystification—we were to say: "It must be a miracle. There is no scientific explanation. It's got to be supernatural."[14]

One interesting thing about this depiction, however, is that it does not seem borne out in the academic literature. Note that several times in the quotations above Dawkins claims that creationists *assume by default* God must be the cause for any event that cannot currently be explained scientifically. Even if we expand the target beyond creationists (generally conceived as promoting a young earth made by God in six days a few thousand years ago) and apply it to anyone who argues for God from lacunae in science, we generally find reasoning that does not match up to the god-of-the-gaps caricature we are given. Sometimes people argue that there are features of the world unexplained by science but explainable in terms of God, but that is not the same as assuming by default that God, and *only* God, can explain those things. Simply put, there are almost no credible cases of Christian experts who employ the gap argument the way it is presented here for ridicule. It is interesting to note that during Dawkins's diatribe he refers only to fictional accounts or imaginary mash-ups of the argument, not actual arguments deployed by respected Christian scholars.

---

12. Richard Dawkins, *The God Delusion* (London: Black Swan, 2016), 151.
13. Dawkins, *The God Delusion*, 153.
14. Dawkins, *The God Delusion*, 154.

His are distortions—amalgams of the worst features of bad arguments he has encountered, reimagined, and put into his own words to make his opponents look as unreasonable as possible.

Second, we have a reasonable tendency to suspect that strange or unusual events are caused by agents. Even if there were evolutionary or survival reasons for having this propensity, that by itself would not show that such beliefs are false (the subject of future chapters). Why should we assume as a matter of scientific prolegomena that unusual natural events, or even the regular features of the natural world, *cannot* be agent-caused? Before we start doing science, can we know ahead of time that no intelligent mind is behind the structures we are going to study? It seems that the only way we could know that is if we have reason to think the only things that exist are the very natural objects we are setting out to study. But how could science show us that? That is a philosophical presupposition, not a scientific conclusion. As C. S. Lewis said:

> Nature gives most of her evidence in answer to the questions we ask her. Here, as in the courts, the character of the evidence depends on the shape of the examination, and a good cross-examiner can do wonders. He will not indeed elicit falsehoods from an honest witness. But, in relation to the total truth in the witness's mind, the structure of the examination is like a stencil. It determines how much of that total truth will appear and what pattern it will suggest.[15]

What we find will be a function of what we look for and the tools we use to look for it. As with anything, it is imperative that we understand what our tools can do—and equally important to understand what they cannot do. The interrogations of science only pertain to empirical questions, so the only portion of the truth that will appear under that cross-examination will come through the senses and what they observe.

---

15. C. S. Lewis, *The Discarded Image: An Introduction to Medieval and Renaissance Literature* (Cambridge: Cambridge University Press, 1964), 222–23.

A third observation is that the objection against god-of-the-gaps reasoning is mostly irrelevant, because religious belief is rarely rooted in such arguments anyway. If individuals accept Judaism, it is most likely because they believe God really did reveal himself uniquely to Israel. The story of the Old Testament rings true to them. If people embrace Islam, it is most likely because they think the Qur'an faithfully preserves a message from Allah. They think that claim has the air of authenticity. If a person follows Christianity, it is likely because he or she accepts what is said about Jesus Christ in the New Testament. These beliefs might spring from a vague sense of the divine, or a gut feeling that there is a higher power, or some other form of emotional, intuitive, or intellectual conviction, but those beliefs need not be—and, I think, usually are not—the result of deductive reasoning from explanatory gaps in science to God. Gap arguments might be used *ex post facto* to help justify belief, but they are almost never its cause. In general, belief in God is not posited merely to explain unexplained natural phenomena. As British author Terry Eagleton so charmingly put it, "Believing that religion is a botched attempt to explain the world [is] like seeing ballet as a botched attempt to run for a bus."[16]

But Aren't There Conflicts?

But the fact is, there are undeniably conflicts sometimes between scientists and believers. Though often based in misunderstanding and poor reasoning, they happen. When we review the cases of Galileo, Newton, and Darwin—or look ahead to current work in brain research—a clear trend emerges. When there are conflicts between scientific and religious communities, there is nearly always an underlying central issue: the explanation of data. The debate is not usually over what the data *are*, but what they *mean*. Science is popularly thought of as being purely objective, intel-

---

16. Terry Eagleton, *Reason, Faith, and Revolution: Reflections on the God Debate* (New Haven, CT: Yale University Press, 2010), 50.

lectually neutral, and dispassionately committed only to the gathering of facts that speak for themselves, and therefore there is no need for interpretation by its practitioners—like Spock coldly reasoning in an emotional and philosophical vacuum. If that were so, there would simply be nothing to disagree about.

Nearly all philosophers of science would disagree with that depiction, though, and it is worth pausing to discuss one of the reasons they would demur: something known as the Duhem-Quine thesis.[17] According to this proposition, scientific hypotheses do not come to us free-floating, separated from other underlying philosophical commitments. They are always situated against a large array of background beliefs, which consist partly of other observations, partly of other empirical hypotheses, and partly of metaphysical and epistemological philosophical propositions. The thesis states that no single hypothesis can be isolated and either decisively refuted or confirmed by experimental data because of that web of background beliefs.

Suppose some scientific hypothesis h entails that a certain result r will come from some experiment e. That is, *h implies r*. When e is performed, however, suppose that the opposite of the expected result obtains: e yields $\sim r$ instead of the anticipated result r, apparently refuting h by a logical inference known as *modus tollens*.[18] But that inference may be too hasty because one never simply has h and h alone as a driving hypothesis. Every hypothesis is nestled within a set of background assumptions b such that the argument above is represented without a key variable in place.

For example, Psalm 96:10 says, "The world is established; it shall never be moved." Galileo's observational data might not exactly refute that claim but instead disconfirm some background assumptions that led medievalists to suppose that the Bible insists on geocentrism. That is, instead of Galileo refuting the Bible, he

---

17. Named for the work of Pierre Duhem and W. V. O. Quine, though the thesis as usually presented does not come directly from the writings of either man, and it is possible that neither of them would actually endorse it.

18. A common form of syllogism: If A then B; not B; therefore not A.

might only have refuted the belief that verses like Psalm 96:10 were astronomical claims meant to endorse Ptolemaic cosmology. If we consider and include background beliefs, which are often unnoticed or unintentional, a complete version would have (*h* & *b*) imply *r*. Then if ~*r* is the result, we cannot conclusively determine whether the experiment shows ~*h* or instead ~*b*. Thus, the result ~*r* might simply refute something within the vast set of (possibly unnoticed) background assumptions. This leads to a real difficulty: the practical, and even theoretical, impossibility of elucidating all of *b* means there can be no complete and conclusive refutation of any specific scientific hypothesis. Thus, as a matter of logic, almost any set of observations can be retained in the face of apparently disconfirming experimental data if one is willing to make enough tweaks to other beliefs somewhere else in the background.

At a certain point, however, modifications to the background assumptions start to seem unreasonable to most people. For example, one modification could be to reject the existence of an external world—or indeed of anything else at all. One could adopt solipsism, the belief that only I exist and everything else is in my imagination. This would certainly open up the door to accommodate all kinds of data, but at a price most of us think is exorbitant. The problem is that there is no clear criterion for when a background belief should be altered. When Ernest Rutherford fired alpha particles at a thin sheet of gold foil to measure their deflection, some showed an angle greater than ninety degrees. He said: "It was quite the most incredible event that has ever happened to me in my life. It was almost as incredible as if you fired a 15-inch shell at a piece of tissue paper and it came back and hit you."[19] What made it so startling was that he had a model of the atom in mind that turned out to be totally wrong, so it was that background belief—the so-called plum pudding model of the

19. E. N. da C. Andrade, *Rutherford and the Nature of the Atom* (Garden City, NY: Doubleday, 1964), 111.

atom—that needed to be changed and replaced with the model we are all so familiar with today. Similarly, the paucity of transitional species in the fossil record led evolutionists not to abandon Darwin's theory but instead to reject his gradualism, which predicted a smooth record of intermediaries to be trapped in the rocks. The lesson from all this is that there are no hard and fast rules that tell us when a background belief should be changed or a hypothesis abandoned, leaving it, to some extent, up to our judgment and the consensus of our peers.

At the end of this discussion it may be helpful to return to the story shared at the beginning of this chapter. Despite my appeals, my friend Mike is still an atheist. But as a result of our conversations, he no longer thinks that his atheism is required or even justified by the findings of modern science. He understands that belief in God does not need to be identified with prescientific ignorance and a desperate search for explanations of mysterious natural events. He agrees that there is no fundamental conflict between science and Christianity. When a believer and an unbeliever can agree on such important questions despite their deep worldview differences, significant progress in the perennial science-religion dialogue has indeed been made. The conflict model, while sometimes noting real and important differences between believers and unbelievers, usually only confuses the actual issues and misrepresents the locus of disagreement.

In the next chapter we will consider other approaches to understanding the science-religion relationship that do not make the common mistake of pitting them as enemies.

3

Science and Christianity (2)

Strangers or Friends?

As we saw in the last chapter, the tension between science and religion is often misunderstood and overblown. In fact, there is so much misinformation and distortion that it might be best to move to a different model altogether, one that does not fundamentally characterize the relationship as hostile. In this chapter we will explore two such alternatives: one that depicts them as strangers, and one as partners.

Science and Religion as Strangers

On the "strangers" telling of things, science and religion operate in two different spheres, making declarations that are really irrelevant to each other. We can call this the "two-realms" view. On this account, science and religion attend to unrelated issues, and the answers each gives have no implications for the other field. Science pertains to the classification of empirical observations, but religion pertains to ethics, ritual, and propositions that have no empirical entailments (such as the assertion that a divine Being exists).

Unlike conflict approaches, where religious claims and scientific claims are seen to contradict each other, this description makes scientific declarations exempt from religious scrutiny and vice versa. Karl Barth, a leading religious figure of the twentieth century, espoused this view. In a letter to his niece, Barth said, "Has no one explained to you in your seminar that one can as little compare the biblical creation story and a scientific theory like that of evolution as one can compare, shall we say, an organ and a vacuum-cleaner—that there can be as little question of harmony between them as of contradiction?"[1] Barth's claim is that a gulf separates science and religion. Their work is unrelated.

Perhaps the most notable scientist to promote this view was paleontologist Stephen Jay Gould. Regarding the relationship between science and religion, Gould said that conflict and agreement are impossible: "No such conflict should exist because each subject has a legitimate magisterium, or domain of teaching authority—and these magisteria do not overlap (the principle that I would like to designate as NOMA, or 'nonoverlapping magisteria')." NOMA affirms that each discipline has an area of inquiry, but denies that they might deal with the same topics. "The net of science," Gould argued, "covers the empirical realm: what is the universe made of (fact) and why does it work this way (theory). The net of religion extends over questions of moral meaning and value. These two magisteria do not overlap."[2] There is no conflict because there is no possibility of addressing the same questions.

One way of distinguishing between the realms of inquiry is with the "faith versus fact" distinction. Typically, the characterization is that faith is belief without evidence, or even belief in the

---

1. Karl Barth, *Letters, 1961–1968*, ed. Jürgen Fangmeier and Hinrich Stoevesandt, trans. and ed. Geoffrey W. Bromiley (Grand Rapids, MI: Eerdmans, 1981), 184.
2. Stephen Jay Gould, "Two Separate Domains," in *Philosophy of Religion*, 5th ed., ed. Michael Peterson, William Hasker, Bruce Reichenbach, and David Basinger (New York: Oxford University Press, 2014), 541.

presence of what could be taken as decisively refuting evidence. Facts, on the other hand, are supposed to be what is tangible and certain. Religious or theological commitments are faith commitments on this position, whereas the claims of science are factual (even if they are possibly wrong and open for revision in the future). Returning again to Gould, he considers the claim that the human species evolved "a factual issue under the magisterium of science," and the claim that we are given a soul by God "a theological notion under the magisterium of religion."[3]

But this apparently straightforward depiction is rife with difficulties. First of all, in normal conversation people do not usually distinguish between "*F* is a fact" and "*F* is true." We usually use "is true" and "is a fact" interchangeably. Therefore, if it is true that Thursday follows Wednesday, for example, it is a fact that Thursday follows Wednesday. But maybe ordinary language is masking an important distinction (it sometimes does), so let us consider a few possible attempts at clarifying the terms.

What Are Facts?

Suppose we were to define facts this way: *F* is a fact if and only if *F* is obviously true. Will that work to sort the magisteria into their proper buckets? Alas, it will not do, for many things that are taken as facts are far from obvious. The fact that apparently solid bodies consist almost completely of empty space is something taught us by atomic theory from our mothers' knees; but it is far from obvious from my own experience of tables and chairs that the particles composing them are exceedingly tiny and fantastically far apart relative to their sizes. Being obviously true won't work as the criterion for being a fact.

Maybe we could try something else. Suppose what we mean by "*F* is a fact" is something that appeals to authority and expertise: "*F* is true and experts agree that *F* is true." In that case, though,

---

3. Gould, "Two Separate Domains," 542.

if the term "experts" doesn't apply only to scientific experts, the claims of religious experts could count as facts as well, and if they all agree that God exists, it would be a factual claim. Why confine expertise only to science? Many people will often admit that Jesus (and maybe Confucius and Buddha and a few others) have a kind of "spiritual genius" and see things the rest of us tend to miss. What about artistic or musical expertise—why should those be excluded? But if we open the door to those things, the distinction fails to get Gould what he is after. If it can only mean "scientific experts," then the definition is ad hoc and circular.

Let's try again. When people contrast fact with faith, they often mean "F is a fact if F is empirically verifiable." Are we now closing in on the quarry? This seems like it could finally provide the scientific heft we need. Yet this approach has difficulties as well. To start, perhaps not surprisingly, there is controversy over what counts as being empirically verifiable. Philosophers of science influenced by Karl Popper argue that scientific claims are refutable but never verifiable. Other philosophers of science argue that scientific claims are verifiable but usually only indirectly. For example, that there were no humans on earth a billion years ago is not something we can directly view because we cannot go back a billion years in time to observe it. The evidence for there being no humans then is indirect, though still empirical. There is also the problem touched on earlier about the nature of many fundamental and indispensable scientific claims that cannot be verified, such as Newton's first law of motion. That law requires impossible conditions: an object that is not subject to any external forces. Nowhere in the universe can that condition be found, so the law cannot be verified but can only be shown to be reasonable with approximations. Many other idealized versions of laws (such as the *ideal gas law*) also describe conditions impossible to meet. Surely such laws are meant to be factual and well established by experience. The point is not that such laws should be rejected, but it should be kept in mind that they are never directly or completely confirmed either.

What Is Faith?

Additionally, there is still the problem of defining faith. What is the supposed difference between fact and faith, and how does it separate religion from science? Simply stating that "*F* is a matter of faith" means "*F* is not a fact" will not do; certainly some faith claims are at least possibly true, and if they are possibly true, they are arguably possibly facts. If Jesus healed a man born blind, then it is a fact that the man was able to see afterward. The acceptance of that claim may require some faith, but the claim itself is a factual one.

Maybe, then, the distinction has to do with being supported by evidence: "*F* is a matter of faith" means "*F* is unsupported by evidence."[4] If this is said of religious beliefs, however, it is not always true, and not even more obviously the case than scientific beliefs. For example, there is the evidence of testimony in favor of the claim that Jesus rose from the dead. One typically allows testimony to serve as evidence for a belief (for example, Jones believes that his friend Smith is at the store because Smith's wife told him so, and she is not known to lie or be wrong about such things). Or, consider the arguments offered in favor of theism: the cosmological argument, the teleological argument, the ontological argument, the moral argument, and more are given in support of religious belief. Those certainly count as rational support and evidence. Thus, it would be false that there is no evidence for religious claims.

Perhaps we should retreat to saying "*F* is a matter of faith" means "*F* is insufficiently supported by evidence." But it is very difficult to settle on a good definition of "insufficiently." William Clifford famously claimed, "It is wrong always, everywhere, and for anyone, to believe anything upon insufficient evidence."[5] But

---

4. Or even stronger and more polemical, Richard Dawkins says: "Faith is the great cop-out, the great excuse to evade the need to think and evaluate evidence. Faith is belief in spite of, even perhaps because of, the lack of evidence" (address, Edinburgh International Science Festival, April 15, 1992).

5. William Kingdon Clifford, *The Ethics of Belief* (1877; repr., New York: Prometheus, 1999), 77.

what is the evidence in support of such a claim? Which experiment establishes it? And if it is not subject to that sort of support, is it simply a matter of accepting the claim on faith, and therefore is it epistemically disrespectable—or even morally wrong, as Clifford argues? The line between fact and faith is not clear and bright.

Granted, one can distinguish between claims that are generally agreed upon—for instance, that there are material objects—and those that are more controversial—for instance, that Moses led the Israelites through the Red Sea. But if the separation of fact from faith just amounts to separating less widely accepted premises from more widely accepted ones, one could carry that separation out in many ways with unexpected, and unwanted, results that diminish the supposed authority of science. If we take a poll across our society, what if the result is that very few people believe that particles can behave as waves, as quantum mechanics implies, but many people believe that God exists? As we discussed earlier regarding a poll about evolution, this approach would even make naturalistic evolution false, since only about one in eight people accept it as a theory. That hardly seems like the way to decide these cases.

Furthermore, even if some religious claims are unsupported by direct evidence, that does not put religion in a different category from science, for science also depends on beliefs unsupported by direct evidence. *That my clear sensations represent the world accurately* and *that my strong memories are generally reliable* are not claims supported by evidence; any evidence that would be cited as supportive of the claims would be supportive only if the claims are already known to be true. The same is true of many propositions assumed by scientists: that knowledge of the world is possible, or that scientific explanations should refer only to natural causes, or that all that exists is the material world. These propositions are no more supported by empirical evidence than their contraries, that knowledge of the world is impossible, or that scientific explanations may invoke God as a cause, or that the material world is not all that exists. Scientists make use of the rules of logic, which are not established scientifically. They reason based on induction, by which it is impossible to achieve the level of certainty they sometimes present themselves as reaching. Thus, it can be argued, science makes many claims unsupported by evidence and perhaps unsupportable by evidence. One ongoing challenge, then, for advocates of the two-realms views such as NOMA is to give clear markers that can be used to delimit the magisteria.

Not Quite NOMA

Furthermore, despite his claim that the magisteria do not overlap, Gould is faced with this very challenge of explaining why religious and scientific claims at least *seem* at times to be at odds. While the conflicts between science and religion are often exaggerated or wrongly depicted, our experience is that there sometimes is genuine disagreement. If there is no overlap of magisteria, however, disagreement should be completely absent.

Indeed, Gould himself even recognizes that there are such areas of contention. There is not a wide gulf separating science and religion,

> but, in fact, the two magisteria bump right up against each other, interdigitating in wondrously complex ways along their joint border. Many of our deepest questions call upon aspects of both magisteria for different parts of a full answer—and the sorting of legitimate domains can become quite complex and difficult.[6]

Again, however, it is hard to understand what "bumping against each other" and "interdigitating" would mean without any overlap whatsoever.

When Gould reports that he is looking forward to seeing how the Catholic Church will "celebrate nature's factuality" and

---

6. Gould, "Two Separate Domains," 542.

begin its "interesting discussion of the theological implications" of evolution,[7] the problem becomes acute. Under what circumstances could there be *theological* implications for evolution? Gould says that the primary concern of religion is "moral meaning and value," but science is about empirical observations. For there to be theological implications from empirical observations, however, there must be a logical connection between an empirical claim and a theological claim. But a logical connection can join the two propositions only if the truth of one is connected to the truth of the other. Perhaps his theory should change its name from NOMA to SOMA: "somewhat overlapping magisteria." It seems that keeping science and religion totally separated, whether by the NOMA approach or by drawing a line between "fact" and "faith," will be difficult if not impossible.

Science and Religion as Partners

The above examples serve to illustrate a serious deficiency with "strangers" approaches to the interaction between science and religion: at best they oversimplify the relationship, and at worst they mischaracterize it. But what would it mean to say that science and religion are partners? What does it mean to say that there is harmony? When considering this question, Ian Barbour broke a lot of new ground in his scholarly work discussing the relationship between science and religion. He described different modes of integration, two of which I will touch on here: natural theology and theology of nature.[8]

Natural Theology

The task of natural theology is to use an understanding of nature to support belief in God, familiar examples being the cosmological argument, the teleological argument, and the argument from

---

7. Gould, "Two Separate Domains," 543.
8. Ian G. Barbour, *When Science Meets Religion* (San Francisco: Harper One, 2000), chap. 1.

consciousness. In cosmological arguments—for example, the *kalam* version of William Lane Craig—the scientific consensus that the cosmos had a beginning is used to point to a Creator since, the argument alleges, nothing can come into being without a cause. Teleological arguments point to the orderliness and complexity of nature to conclude that a designer is most likely behind it. In this vein, Francis Bacon argued in his essay "Of Atheism" that recent advances in science (known then as experimental philosophy), which supplanted the scholastic approach to physics with its four elements, accorded well with belief in God's existence. He said:

> God never wrought miracle to convince atheism, because His ordinary works convince it. It is true that a little philosophy [that is, science] inclineth man's mind to atheism; but depth in philosophy bringeth men's minds about to religion: for while the mind of man looketh upon second causes scattered, it may sometimes rest in them, and go no farther; but when it beholdeth the chain of them confederate and linked together, it must needs fly to Providence and Deity. Nay, even that school which is most accused of atheism doth most demonstrate religion. For it is a thousand times more credible, that four mutable elements, and one immutable fifth essence duly and eternally placed, need no God; than that an army of infinite small portions, or seeds unplaced, should have produced this order and beauty without a divine Marshall.[9]

According to some advocates of Intelligent Design, the origin of life and the presence of irreducibly complex systems are thought to be inexplicable, or at least highly improbable, without divine agency behind them. Likewise, Robin Collins and Peter van Inwagen argue that the apparent fine-tuning of important physical constants is so unlikely, given the range of possible values—most of which would lead to an uninhabitable universe—

---

9. Francis Bacon, *Essays and New Atlantis* (Roslyn, NY: Walter J. Black, 1969), 66–67.

that design by God is the best explanation. Regarding consciousness, Richard Swinburne and J. P. Moreland claim that there is no
satisfying naturalistic way to account for the ability of humans
to think, since matter on its own would be incapable of generat-
ing thought. They claim that consciousness requires something
that transcends "the web of physical laws." Along those same
lines, Alvin Plantinga and Victor Reppert state that our cognitive
faculties can be considered reliable only if they were aimed at
producing true beliefs, which would require an ends-based process
of development that cannot be accounted for by random varia-
tions and natural selection alone (we will discuss these last two
arguments in later chapters). Thus, with all of these arguments
science and religion would be in harmony because science is seen
as benefiting from having God as the ultimate explanation of the
phenomena we observe.

Theology of Nature

The quest by some for a theology of nature is yet one more important approach. Natural theology argues that God's existence
is likely or even necessary, given the way the world is; a theology
of nature starts with a set of theological convictions, arrived at
independently of science, and seeks to understand science in that
theological context. In this way, too, science and religion are seen
as in harmony, not because they need each other but because they
can illuminate each other. The sources of knowledge are independent of each other for the most part, but theological doctrines
and scientific discoveries should end up being compatible. For
thinkers like Arthur Peacocke, Wolfhart Pannenberg, Robert Russell, Nancey Murphy, and John Polkinghorne, scientific advances
serve as fillips for theological reflection. An example is quantum
mechanics, especially as the standard interpretation introduces
the idea of objective indeterminism in nature. If nature is really
indeterministic and random at the quantum level, then there is a
new question to reflect on theologically: how does God order the

universe and know the future if the current state of things appears to leave a variety of possible futures open? And what would it look like for God to be the "determiner of indeterminacies"?

These contemporary approaches to a theology of nature are not new. Strains of this thinking can be found at least as far back as Thomas Aquinas, and they become more and more prevalent in the eighteenth and nineteenth centuries. Benjamin Franklin showed that lightning has a physical cause, but he would not conclude that it occurs outside of divine providence. Puritan minister and author Cotton Mather said that earthquakes have physical causes but that they are still rightly thought of as caused by God too: "[Natural] causes are still under the government of Him that is the God of Nature."[10] In discussing evolution, evangelical theologian and staunch defender of biblical inerrancy B. B. Warfield said that divine creation "is in no way inconsistent with . . . a complete system of natural causation"[11] such as one would find with evolution. People like Galileo, Gassendi, Kepler, Descartes, Newton, Pascal, Boyle, and many more have sought the harmonization of science and religion.

Protestant Christian Reformer John Calvin encouraged Christians to study nature through scientific investigation, because science was the study of God's handiwork. As such, Calvin believed it both honored the Creator and taught creatures about the one who made them.

> There is a need of art and of more exacting toil in order to investigate the motion of the stars, to determine their assigned stations, to measure their intervals, to note their properties. . . . Likewise, in regard to the structure of the human body

---

10. Ronald L. Numbers, "Science without God," in *When Science and Christianity Meet*, ed. David C. Lindberg and Ronald L. Numbers (Chicago: University of Chicago Press, 2003), 271.

11. B. B. Warfield, review of *Darwinism To-day*, by Vernon L. Kellogg, *Princeton Theological Review* 6, no. 4 (1908): 649. See also David N. Livingstone and Mark A. Noll, "B. B. Warfield (1851–1921): A Biblical Inerrantist as Evolutionist," *Isis* 91, no. 2 (2000): 283–94.

one must have the greatest keenness in order to weigh, with Galen's skill, its articulation, symmetry, beauty, and use.[12]

This is because "the Lord represents both himself and his everlasting Kingdom in the mirror of his works with very great clarity."[13] Similar statements are common from countless authors, such as Charles Hodge, Asa Gray, W. B. Carpenter, W. H. Dallinger, and many more who describe natural laws as the manners of God's acting, so that discovery of them by no means pushes God off the stage but merely illuminates the manner in which he governs nature. Religious thinkers who advocate a theology of nature thus try to bring their religious beliefs and science together to further shape both their doctrine and their understanding of the natural world by reflecting theologically on science.

God and Causation

One more distinction needs to be developed. Many Christian thinkers have insisted that the bifurcation between *events with natural causes* and *events with supernatural causes* is for convenience only and does not reflect ultimate reality. Consider these verses from Psalm 104:

> You make springs gush forth in the valleys;
>   they flow between the hills;
> they give drink to every beast of the field;
>   the wild donkeys quench their thirst.
> Beside them the birds of the heavens dwell;
>   they sing among the branches.
> From your lofty abode you water the mountains;
>   the earth is satisfied with the fruit of your work.
>
> You cause the grass to grow for the livestock
>   and plants for man to cultivate,

---

12. John Calvin, *Institutes of the Christian Religion*, ed. John T. McNeill, trans. Ford Lewis Battles (Philadelphia: Westminster, 1960), 1.5.2.
13. Calvin, *Institutes*, 1.5.11.

    that he may bring forth food from the earth
        and wine to gladden the heart of man,
    oil to make his face shine
        and bread to strengthen man's heart. (vv. 10–15)

In Matthew 5:45, Jesus says, "[God] makes his sun rise on the evil and on the good, and sends rain on the just and on the unjust." Thus, Jesus was saying that God is one who *acts*. He "will neither slumber nor sleep" (Ps. 121:4). Jesus also said, "My Father is always at his work to this very day, and I too am working" (John 5:17 NIV). When assuring people of God's constant care for them and awareness of every facet of their lives, Jesus said, "Are not two sparrows sold for a penny? And not one of them will fall to the ground apart from your Father" (Matt. 10:29). Even the minute details of life are within God's plan and carried out by his activity.

In Colossians, Paul says that Jesus Christ "is before all things, and in him all things hold together" (1:17). The world was not simply wound up and left to go on its own. Rather, it has its being and character completely through the ongoing work of God. The author of Hebrews proclaims that all things were made by God through Christ, and then declares, "He is the radiance of the glory of God and the exact imprint of his nature, and he upholds the universe by the word of his power" (Heb. 1:3). The universe is, moment by moment, the product of God's sustaining and continuing creative work—God is always and everywhere *acting*. All of these verses, and many more, speak to the immanence of God even in what we take to be ordinary natural events. They affirm the total dependence of creation at all times on the sustaining work of God the Creator.

Three Models

There are three main ways of modeling God's action in the regular lawlike events of the world. The first is *mere conservationism*, according to which God "acts" in nature mainly by being the original source of it. After creating, God preserves things in existence, but when causal interactions occur, the natural objects involved really do cause what happens. While God in some sense acts in the normal course of nature by sustaining things in existence, they have a fairly high level of autonomy and in some meaningful way really do act on their own. God is merely an indirect or remote cause of what happens in the world. That has not proved to be a robust enough view of God's role in natural events, though, so most Christian philosophers and theologians have opted for something stronger, such as the next two approaches.

The second model is *concurrence*, according to which the behavior of natural objects is caused both by those objects *and* by God. So, when a created thing causes something to happen, it really is a genuine contributing cause, but God is too—he acts in concurrence with the natural object.

The third model is *occasionalism*, according to which God is the only and sole cause of all nonmental physical events (leaving room for at least the possibility of other mental-agent causes). Natural objects really end up making no contribution to the causal goings-on in the world, God simply uses the occasion of things being in a certain relationship as the initiating condition for his own actions. These two descriptions of divine action have been the dominant views in Christian theology for many centuries.

With any of those three models, especially concurrence and occasionalism, a proper approach to understanding the causal relation between God and the world is never going to be based on finding little chinks in the scientists' armor and trying to exploit them to invoke God as a necessary stopgap. It is rather to put God at the center of causal nexus of everything that happens, at all times and places, whether apparently supernatural and miraculous or following the familiar patterns we build our lives around. Having natural explanations does not eliminate a divine explanation. We should not fall prey to the false dichotomy that explanations must refer *either* to God *or* to natural laws. We can overlay one on top of the other—explanations that refer to natural laws are built on the foundational proposition that God is always acting. The whole system of nature at every moment is the outworking of God's creative and sustaining activity. There is no ultimate separation between natural events and God's actions.

This point is also misunderstood by many scientists. For example, Neil deGrasse Tyson, high-profile astrophysicist and popular science writer, also (like Dawkins) accuses believers of using god-of-the-gaps arguments whenever there is something science does not currently understand. But in doing so, he misrepresents the people he quotes for support and demonstrates his ignorance of what they really mean. In an article titled "The Perimeter of Ignorance,"[14] Tyson says there is "a boundary where scientists face a choice: invoke a deity or continue the quest for knowledge." Tyson proceeds to quote Ptolemy, Isaac Newton, Galileo, and other scientists who wrote in praise of God's marvelous works in creation. To Tyson, the meaning of these paeans was to invoke God to explain the unexplainable, but this is not what they were doing.

For example, Tyson quotes Christiaan Huygens saying:

> I suppose nobody will deny but that there's somewhat more of Contrivance, somewhat more of Miracle in the production and growth of Plants and Animals than in lifeless heaps of inanimate Bodies. . . . For the finger of God, and the Wisdom of Divine Providence, is in them much more clearly manifested than in the other.

Tyson thinks that Huygens invokes God simply because Huygens does not understand the origins of life with the same scientific detail that he understands the structure of the solar system. But if what I said before is right—if one can see God's handiwork *at the same time* as one sees the operations of natural law—then Tyson is

---

14. Neil deGrasse Tyson, "The Perimeter of Ignorance," *Natural History*, November 2005, 28–34.

tripping over the same false dichotomy discussed earlier. Huygens is noting that there is more wisdom manifested in the formation and superintendence of living things than in that of inanimate things, but that is plain and undeniable. It is not an appeal to ignorance but a statement of the obvious. Or, when Newton says about God, "We know him only by his most wise and excellent contrivances of things, and final causes; we admire him for his perfections; but we reverence and adore him on account of his dominion,"[15] he is not, as Tyson avers, invoking God because he needs an explanation; he is praising the Maker of all things for his divine skill and craftsmanship. The two are not mutually exclusive.

In reflecting on the origin of natural laws and the orderliness of nature, British writer G. K. Chesterton saw clearly that the patterns we see in nature are really patterns of God's acting. But he was also aware that the deists, who saw God as Creator but not the continual ground of all being, considered this approach to understanding God's relation to his creation as threatening tedium. They thought such ceaseless activity was unfitting for God—it was too repetitious, too boring. It was, in fact, beneath his dignity. But Chesterton saw it differently and put it this way:

> Because children have abounding vitality, because they are in spirit fierce and free, therefore they want things repeated and unchanged. They always say, "Do it again"; and the grown-up person does it again until he is nearly dead. For grown-up people are not strong enough to exult in monotony. But perhaps God is strong enough to exult in monotony. It is possible that God says every morning, "Do it again" to the sun; and every evening, "Do it again" to the moon. It may not be automatic necessity that makes all daisies alike; it may be that God makes every daisy separately, but has never got tired of

---

15. Isaac Newton, "General Scholium," in *The Mathematical Principles of Natural Philosophy*, trans. Andrew Motte, vol. 2 (London, 1729), 391, the Newton Project (website), accessed November 4, 2019, http://www.newtonproject.ox.ac.uk/view/texts/normalized/NATP00056.

making them. It may be that He has the eternal appetite of infancy; for we have sinned and grown old, and our Father is younger than we.[16]

Chesterton's evocative picture is of a God who delights in his creation and, for that reason, upholds it moment by moment through the word of his power.

As we think about the relationship between science and religion in the following pages of this book, this will be the underlying metaphysical and theological framework. God is acting. God is the Creator. Do we have a history? It was brought about by God. Are we built a certain way, with tendencies to believe or act in common ways? Those patterns result from God's divine design plan. Who we are—including how we got here and where we're going—is entirely because God made us to be that way. Our brains are a fascinating part of the picture, but we must remember not to lose the forest for the trees.

We will think of science as a way to underscore and illuminate God's role as Creator, and the Christian worldview as what can give science an intellectual, aesthetic, and moral framework in which to flourish. According to this approach, science and religion will not conflict if they are done properly and from the right perspective, because they represent two sides of the same coin in describing all of reality, physical and spiritual. Much of the data is, in and of itself, neutral and open to multiple interpretations, as we shall continue to see. But looking at the data another way, we can see strong support for traditional Christian beliefs. We will be adopting a perspective that is reminiscent of C. S. Lewis's reflections: "I believe in Christianity as I believe that the sun has risen: not only because I see it, but because by it I see everything else."[17] It is by and through a biblical lens that we will look at the enthralling world of the brain.

---

16. G. K. Chesterton, *Orthodoxy* (San Francisco: Ignatius, 1995), 65–66.
17. C. S. Lewis, "They Asked for a Paper," in *Is Theology Poetry?* (London: Geoffrey Bles, 1962), 164–65.

4

Evolutionary Explanations
for Belief in God

While the spiritual nature of humanity has certainly been a target for materialist scientists and secular thinkers, it is by no means the only target. In dealing with the brain, its structures, and its functions, the researcher or even any casual observer is confronted with an indisputable fact: people are, in general, incurably religious. For as long as we have been able to tell, beliefs about gods and spirits have populated nearly every culture at nearly every time. Yet many people who study the brain are convinced that the time has come to jettison not only beliefs in souls but all such religious beliefs—that they have no place in the modern world but are merely barnacles still clinging to the hull from the eons we spent moored in the intellectually stagnant waters of the ignorant past.

Why Belief?

From the standpoint of secular science, the persistence of religion is an evolutionary puzzle. After all, unlike beliefs in lions and tigers and tables and chairs, belief in gods or spirits does not come to us directly through the gates of the senses. We do not see God or the souls of dead ancestors. The fact that religious beliefs are so widespread and persistent is astonishing. To a naturalist, it represents a massive failure of our cognitive equipment that so many of us would be so deluded for so long. So why do we believe?

There are myriad attempts to explain the origins of religious belief, and efforts to do so using only naturalistic means have been around for millennia. However, there is a new kid on the block. Cognitive science of religion (or CSR) is a recent multi-pronged, interdisciplinary approach to understanding the development and persistence of religious belief. Leading figures in the field come from a wide variety of backgrounds, including psychology, neuroscience, anthropology, sociology, and philosophy. These approaches only really began in the 1990s, and the expression "cognitive science of religion" was coined by Fuller Seminary psychology professor Justin Barrett in 2000.[1] Despite the academic diversity of its practitioners, a set of common convictions has emerged. Here is one helpful taxonomy of those central CSR principles about religious beliefs:

(1) [Religious beliefs] are counter-intuitive in ways that make them optimally suited for recall and transmission.

(2) They spring from cognitive mechanisms that generate beliefs about agents and agency.

(3) They typically represent the religious entities as minded agents who, because of their counter-intuitive character, stand to benefit us in our attempt to maintain stable relationships in large interacting groups.

(4) They are also inference-rich and thus allow us to generate narratives about them that enhance their memorability,

---

1. Justin L. Barrett, "Exploring the Natural Foundations of Religion," *Trends in Cognitive Sciences* 4, no. 1 (2000): 29–34. We will hear more from Barrett later in this chapter and beyond.

make them attractive as objects of ritual, and increase our affective reaction towards them.[2]

These properties give us a picture of belief formation and transmission that treats religion as a natural phenomenon, emerging organically from our cognitive dispositions paired with widespread, nearly universal human cultural and social practices. Each of them introduces an important idea in CSR, but two in particular are important to understand. We will attend to those first.

Counter-Intuition

The first important notion in CSR that emerges is *counterintuitive* ideas. Since the question is how religious beliefs emerge, it is important to note what distinguishes religious ideas from nonreligious. As we reflect on it, we notice that for most contexts religious beliefs involve agents who are different from us in important ways. They are similar to us in many ways, as well, but different enough that they are noteworthy and memorable. They are like us in having desires, being able to act, having knowledge of what is happening in the world, and so forth; they are different in being invisible or able to pass through walls, or creating objects out of nothing, or being impervious to weapons. Scott Atran and Dan Sperber explain:

> They are generally inconsistent with common-sense knowledge, but not at random: rather, they dramatically contradict basic common-sense assumptions. For instance, they include beliefs about invisible creatures, beliefs about creatures who can transform themselves at will or who can perceive events that are distant in time or space. This flatly contradicts factual, common-sense assumptions about physical, biological, and psychological phenomena. . . . As a result, these beliefs are more likely to be retained and transmitted in a human group

2. David Leech and Aku Visala, "The Cognitive Science of Religion: A Modified Theist Response," *Religious Studies* 47, no. 3 (2011): 301–16.

than random departures from common sense, and thus to become part of the group's culture.

. . . To the extent such violations of category distinctions shake basic notions of ontology, they are attention-arresting, hence memorable. But only to the degree that the resultant impossible worlds remain bridged to the everyday world can information about them be stored and evoked in plausible grades.[3]

Furthermore, the counterintuitive ideas cannot be *too* far from our own experiences, or they will come across as merely bizarre or silly. Consider the famous mockery of Christianity and other traditional religions as the Church of the Flying Spaghetti Monster. The supposed followers, known as "pastafarians," purport to believe in and worship a deity made of spaghetti who has the power of flight, mind control, and creation. No doubt, the inventors think they are making a clever mockery of Christianity and other religions, but the deity they concocted could and would never be taken seriously. There are many reasons for this, but one problem is that a flying monster made of noodles violates too many expectations we have for agents. In the language of CSR, this means it is not *minimally counterintuitive*, as religious ideas tend to be.

How, then, do we get minimally counterintuitive ideas (MCI)? Justin Barrett describes his proposal for the method this way:

Create an MCI in the following way. First, take an ordinary concept, such as "tree," "shoe," or "dog," that meets all of the naturally occurring assumptions of our categorizers and describers. Then violate one of the assumptions. For instance, as a bounded physical object, a tree activates the nonreflective beliefs governing physical objects, including being visible. So make the tree invisible (otherwise a perfectly good tree), and

---

3. Scott Atran and Dan Sperber, "Learning without Teaching: Its Place in Culture," in *Culture, Schooling and Psychological Development*, ed. Liliana Tolchinsky Landsmann (Norwood, NJ: Ablex, 1991), 52.

you have an MCI. Similarly, an MCI may be made by transferring an assumption from another category of things. A shoe, as an artifact (human-made thing), is not assumed to grow or develop. These assumptions deal with living things. Hence, a shoe that grows old and dies would be an MCI, whereas a dog that grows old and dies is ordinary. Constructing MCIs merely consists of either violating a property (or a small number of properties) nonreflectively assumed by categorizers and describers or transferring a property (or a small number of properties) from a different category of things that is nonreflectively assumed for the other category.[4]

The deviations cannot be too far afield from the original expectations for objects of that category, or else it fails to be *minimally* counterintuitive and loses its stickiness. When ideas are minimally counterintuitive, says CSR, they are much more likely to be accepted, remembered, and transmitted. Each of those aspects is critical, for the transmission of an idea—by teaching and preaching, for instance—is what gives the idea staying power in the culture. Without being memorable, an idea will not be transmitted; without being transmitted, it will not endure as a religious notion. CSR says that the sweet spot for memorability and likeliness of transmission is when the idea is minimally counterintuitive.

This does, however, raise an interesting point: on what grounds do we judge these ideas to be counterintuitive? That is, should we agree with the assumption that we have no natural, proper intuitions that correspond to religious ideas but only intuitions that connect us to the material and sensory world? Consider the language of Atran and Sperber above: "They are generally inconsistent with common-sense knowledge." Is that true? What is to rule out the possibility that these ideas are every bit as intuitive as our sensory ideas, as advocates of Reformed epistemology might say? We will pick up this thread again later, but the assumption

---

4. Justin L. Barrett, *Why Would Anyone Believe in God?* (Walnut Creek, CA: AltaMira, 2004), 12.

that religious beliefs are counterintuitive seems already to commit one to a belief about what the world is like and how we are naturally designed to respond to it. If religious belief is instilled in us by God, for example, then religious ideas are not counterintuitive after all, nor would they be "generally inconsistent with common-sense knowledge"—they would be a *part* of such knowledge, not in opposition to it.

Other Minds

Despite that problem, which we will explore in more depth later, the "minimally counterintuitive" criterion is a common one in CSR. The second element we turn to now is that religious beliefs often center on "minded agents." That is, they focus on beings who, like us, have desires, make decisions, and act autonomously. When we encounter rocks and other inanimate objects, we (usually) have no temptation to think that they have *thoughts*. When we encounter other people, we cannot avoid the conclusion that they have thoughts, and we assume that their mental lives and the way they process information as conscious beings are very similar to our own. A lot of work has been done in philosophy on the "problem of other minds," or what justifies us in assuming that other beings have mental lives similar to ours, but we will not enter that controversy now and will assume that we are fully justified in those suppositions.

When we project those things onto others—things in our mental lives that we believe are present in the lives of other people too— we are taking what Daniel Dennett refers to as "the intentional stance." Says Dennett, "To a first approximation, the intentional strategy consists of treating the object whose behavior you want to predict as a rational agent with beliefs and desires and other mental stages exhibiting what Brentano and others call intentionality."[5] The common-thread belief in CSR is that we adopt the intentional

---

5. Daniel C. Dennett, *The Intentional Stance* (Cambridge, MA: MIT Press, 1987), 15.

stance toward the objects of our religious beliefs. We believe that the gods, spirits, or other invisible agents have minds somewhat similar to ours, that they have intentions, and that they are capable of acting on those intentions—particularly in ways that affect our well-being.

There is no uncontroversial explanation for religion in CSR, despite that common core. There are a variety of approaches, and there is not even agreement about how to classify the many approaches on offer. But for a specific example of the treatment of the subject by one of the field's leading researches, let us turn now to one helpful way of dividing up the arguments. Why did religious propensities develop? Why does CSR propose that people are religious?

Four Models from Boyer on Religious Propensities

In his influential book *Religion Explained*, anthropologist and researcher Pascal Boyer (not himself a religious believer) states that "most accounts of the origins of religion emphasize one of the following suggestions: human minds demand explanations, human hearts seek comfort, human society requires order, human intellect is illusion-prone."[6] These broad categories represent the various ways that naturalistic accounts of the origins of religious belief can be classified. Most efforts to say why people are religious make an appeal to one of these supposed benefits of religious belief, things that the believer gets as a reward for believing and participating in the life of the religious community. As such, they provide an evolutionary benefit (the story goes) that ensures their continued propagation and explains why they started in the first place.

Let's peel back the layers and survey the four general approaches Boyer describes.

---

6. Pascal Boyer, *Religion Explained: The Evolutionary Origins of Religious Thought* (New York: Basic Books, 2002), 5.

Human Minds Demand Explanations

The first is that religious beliefs develop in order to explain the unexplainable. We have considered this approach already in an earlier chapter, but additionally Boyer notes that religion, according to this view, is devised to explain natural phenomena, puzzling experiences like dreams or visions, the origin of the world, or the existence of apparently random evil and suffering. In agreeing about the difficulties and inaccuracies with this description I discussed earlier, Boyer flatly denies that religion is there to explain. He does, however, suggest what he labels "a different angle: Religious concepts are probably influenced by the way the brain's inference systems produce explanations without our being aware of it."[7] Note that Boyer calls this an *influence*—not a decisive factor, and not the only one.

This nicely illustrates Boyer's general approach, and he is a good representative of the broader trend in cognitive science of religion to pull in multiple cognitive propensities and systems that operate somewhat independently but cooperatively. According to this kind of explanation, as we shall see, there is no single reason explaining belief—and certainly not a conscious one. As I have argued before, and as Boyer agrees, this is simply not what actually gives rise to belief for almost anyone. Belief arrives through a more organic process than that, and at any rate the extravagance of introducing gods to explain puzzling weather patterns or unknown diseases seems hardly necessary. He notes:

> The mind does not work like one general "let's-review-the-facts-and-get-an-explanation" device. Rather, it comprises lots of specialized explanatory devices, more properly called inference systems, each of which is adapted to particular kinds of events and automatically suggests explanations for these events.[8]

---

7. Boyer, *Religion Explained*, 18.
8. Boyer, *Religion Explained*, 10.

Human Hearts Seek Comfort

With Boyer's second consideration, that human hearts need comfort, there are similar problems. He notes that religion is often supposed to allay the fear of death by promising an afterlife, and to provide comfort when life is difficult—the consolation that there is a plan, and someone good and wise is in control. And undoubtedly the Christian gospel does that. It liberates us from fear, assures us of salvation, promises that history has a direction, and offers us endless life in the joyful presence of our Redeemer. At least two other things are equally clear, however.

First, pagan religions can hardly be described the same way. Most of the history of religious thought and behavior, and many of the current religious systems, are devoid of the promises that come with the good news of Jesus. If religion is supposed to emerge in order to comfort us, for most people now and in history it has not done a very good job.

Second, in addition to those positive aspects, there is an equal amount of discomfort generated by religious belief. One must surrender the idea that life is whatever we want it to be; that wrong behavior carries consequences only if we get caught; that after the grave all accountability is gone and death can offer us the bliss of nonexistence. Depending on how you hold these things to the light, a very different pattern can emerge. Religion can hardly be said to always or even usually offer more comfort than discomfort.

Human Society Requires Order

The third theory is that religion emerges to provide a social structure. For example, inasmuch as religion instills the belief that our ways are watched by an invisible Judge, we are much more likely to play by the moral rules and behave ourselves. Proverbs 5:21 says,

> For a man's ways are before the eyes of the LORD,
>   and he ponders all his paths.

The thought that God is watching is highly motivating, especially when paired with the idea that God is a just Judge, and those who escape punishment on earth for their wrongdoing will nevertheless give account to God at the final judgment. Similarly, those who stay the course and do what is right may fail to get rewarded or even noticed by other people, but there is consolation knowing that obedience will ultimately be praised and rewarded by the God who sees. I will say more about the moral aspect of religion later, and it is not the only aspect of social order that religion helps support. For example, religion helps hold society together through shared celebrations or gatherings. Days of feasting, commemorating important historical religious events, praying together as a family or church or nation—these things all help a people cohere. The role of government is seen in Christian theology as one of the ways God governs his world, and that good citizenship on earth is an aspect of good citizenship in the heavenly kingdom. All of these are benefits of a shared set of religious beliefs. As Boyer says, "Social groups would fall apart if ritual did not periodically reestablish that all members are part of a greater whole."[9]

Again, however, there is a lot more to it than that, and even if all of those benefits really do accrue as a result of religion, that by no means indicates that they developed *for that reason*. There is a fallacy in thinking that the consequences of an action, even if they are foreknown, are the same as the reasons for that action. Suppose a family plans a drive to northern Minnesota to view the unparalleled natural beauty found in our unspoiled wilderness. From where they live, they might calculate that such a trip will burn fifty dollars' worth of gas, but no one would conclude that they made the trip *in order to* spend fifty dollars on fuel. That is a consequence, but not the reason. Furthermore, the need for a common life and some social rhythms to reinforce unity does not entail that those events need to be religious in nature. The Fourth

---

9. Boyer, *Religion Explained*, 15.

of July provides for great unity, as do Thanksgiving, Labor Day, Memorial Day, and other holidays, even though (at least for most people) there is nothing religious about those celebrations.

In addition, once more we can compare Christian belief with many pagan systems and see that the correspondence between good social order and responsible citizenship is by no means a universal implication of religious participation. Some religious systems are highly violent, disruptive, or antisocial in other ways. Does radical Islamic theology promote good social order? Even for religious systems that do not actively undermine order, many are order-neutral and do very little or nothing to support social structure better than nonbelief, or they trade off any benefits for deficits in other ways.

Human Intellect Is Illusion-Prone: Reason Asleep

The fourth proposal is that religion is nothing but a cognitive illusion—a mere chimera that we are finally mature enough to stop believing in. This is what Boyer calls "the sleep of reason: religion as an illusion." As he describes it: "There is a long and respectable tradition of explaining religion as the consequence of a flaw in mental functioning. Because people do not think much or do not think very well, the argument goes, they let all sorts of unwarranted beliefs clutter their mental furniture."[10] The advocates of this position are likely to say things like the following: "People are superstitious. They like the feeling of mystery and magic. Since religious ideas can't be refuted with evidence, they blindly accept them because they don't know any better and it feels good to believe in the mystical." Reason, they say, is simply asleep at the wheel and all kinds of bad ideas are allowed to run rampant.

This argument seems weak, though, for several reasons. It may be true that religious claims are, in some unique ways, unverifiable and unfalsifiable, and also true that they excite the imagination and create feelings of awe and wonder. But is there a general

---

10. Boyer, *Religion Explained*, 28.

principle that all claims with those features are false? Or even more likely false than true? After all, many people report the same sort of feelings of excitement about scientific discoveries; and as we have seen, many "scientific" claims and theories are very far from being verifiable. Does that automatically make them false?

Furthermore, as Boyer acknowledges, "Religion is *not* a domain where anything goes, where any strange belief could appear and get transmitted from generation to generation."[11] As we saw in the discussion of minimally counterintuitive ideas, only beliefs with certain features are likely to have any staying power. Being unusual or exciting to the imagination is neither necessary nor sufficient for belief, and those features are not unique to religious beliefs anyway. People do not believe something simply because someone has said so, or because it is fun to believe it. Again, as Boyer says, "People relax their standards because some thoughts become plausible, not the other way around."[12]

Looking back at the four dominant reasons given as explanations for religion, Boyer notes that "they all fail to tell us why we have religion and why it is the way it is."[13] Each points to something real and worth discussing, but they all miss something too. Granted, they are all very common, even to the point of being bland. They occur throughout history and get recycled as explanations for belief in God by skeptics from the time of ancient Greece to today—even though their proponents seem to think they are saying something original, no matter how many iterations have gone before them. However, these approaches do not dig quite deep enough because they do not explain or account for the mechanisms that lead us to belief to begin with. For example, *why* do we look to invisible divine beings to explain mysterious phenomena rather than just leave them unexplained? Why insist on an explanation instead of accepting them as unexplainable? Or

---

11. Boyer, *Religion Explained*, 29.
12. Boyer, *Religion Explained*, 31.
13. Boyer, *Religion Explained*, 5.

why would we be subject to the religious "illusion" instead of seeing through it or being incredulous and unbelieving? What is it, in other words, that predisposes us to accept religious beliefs at all?

Adaptations?

Much of this debate revolves around two competing ideas about the origin of the mechanisms supposed to generate religious beliefs in the first place. In short, the disagreement is between adaptationists, on one hand, and non-adaptationists (or "spandrelists"), on the other.[14] According to the adaptationists' perspective, the cognitive propensities we have that develop religious beliefs were selected because they somehow or other ended up providing an evolutionary advantage. The primary way evolution moves forward is supposed to be through selecting beneficial changes and ensuring that those get passed on. If the adaptationists are right, religion offers an advantage.

According to the non-adaptationist or spandrel view, the development of religious beliefs was produced by faculties or practices selected for a *different* reason, which ended up producing religious beliefs as an unforeseen and unintended by-product (that's just a figure of speech, of course—evolution is incapable of foreseeing or intending anything). The beliefs themselves would not be adaptive, then, but are only the offshoots of other successful developments in cognition and culture.

Much of the discussion about the origin of religion has traditionally approached it by asking what the advantage to being religious is. Some have argued that religion promotes group cohesion, as we have seen. Other people have argued that religious behavior is adaptive because it makes someone more attractive to potential

---

14. They are named after the architectural features known as spandrels, generally triangular blocks of wood between arches. The tendency is for designers to fill in those features with elaborate carvings. The carvings are just a way to fill in a blank—the "nature abhors a vacuum" principle applied to art. Many of my students fill their notebook margins with similar doodles. The idea is that evolution generates innovative doodles of its own to fill in the ecological blanks.

mates. That is, a religious person is more likely to be conscientious, faithful to his or her spouse, present in raising and providing for children, and in general more likely to be a suitable partner in reproduction. Modern social science research has also borne this out, and many studies show that serious religious engagement is strongly correlated with those traits.

Yet another approach would be that religious people are better equipped to deal with the struggles of life by believing that life has a purpose, that there is someone in charge, and even that death itself will not be the end, but rewards for good behavior and punishment for bad behavior await us all after the grave. As such, religious belief gives one the character traits needed to weather the storms of life and be more likely to come through to the other side successfully. These perspectives and others like them argue that religious belief confers survival and reproductive advantages, and for that reason have been favored by evolution. Friedrich Nietzsche viewed religion as a means for people to gain power over others, enabling them to survive and reproduce better. Karl Marx thought that religion served the poor by offering comfort in the afterlife, and it served the rich by giving them divine and moral authority to control the masses. Sigmund Freud thought we developed religion to deal with the fears and pains of life as a way to be comforted and have our wishes fulfilled. All of these are examples of thinking that religious beliefs exist because they offer a direct benefit.

On the non-adaptationist side, which has been gaining ground and seems to be the more favored approach in CSR, religious beliefs are not directly selected, but just happen to be produced by cognitive mechanisms that *are* directly beneficial on the whole. For example, a car engine gives off heat, but one does not buy a car in order to produce heat by running the engine. Instead, a car is meant to transport us from one point to another. That is why we buy cars—the heat they give off is just a result of their doing the job they were primarily intended to do.

One example of this indirect selection would be supposedly "hyperactive agency detection devices" or HADDs. The thinking here is that we are wired to err on the side of caution, and as a result we might imagine things that aren't there. We know that other people have minds and all that goes with that—plans, desires, intentions, and so forth. But we also know some things, like stones, do not. However, at times it is not clear whether something else has a mind, or whether something happened purely by chance or was the product of an agent. If I hear a tapping noise while lying in bed at night, I might assume that the noise is coming from the ductwork or a tree branch being blown by the wind. But, because there is a chance it might also be an intruder, I would get out of bed to go take a look. When I do that, I am showing my uncertainty about whether an agent is causing something to happen or not. To be safe, though, we might be hardwired to err on the side of agency. When faced with a mysterious process or event, it might be in our interest to assume that an agent is involved.

Because they overreact, though, these agency detection mechanisms are labeled "hyperactive." Consider *pareidolia* as an example—the tendency to see patterns in things when no pattern is really there. When a section of tree bark looks like a face, or a potato chip resembles the Virgin Mary, or we see a face on the moon or in a cloud—these are examples of pareidolia. So the suggestion is that this tendency is at work not only in such cases but whenever we imagine that a being—an intelligent agent with similarities to us—is behind the weather, a disease, or other twists of fortune for good or ill.

Combining these last two ideas so central to CSR—HADDs and memorable minimally counterintuitive concepts—Daniel Dennett gives us this colorful description:

> Put these two ideas together—a hyperactive agent-seeking bias and a weakness for certain sorts of memorable combos—and you get a kind of fiction-generating contraption. Every time

something puzzling happens, it triggers a sort of curiosity star-
tle, a *"Who's there?"* response that starts churning out "hypotheses" of sorts: "Maybe it's Sam, maybe it's a wolf, maybe
it's a falling branch, maybe it's . . . a tree that can walk—*hey,
maybe it's a tree that can walk!*[15]

So, along with many other proponents of the spandrel view,
Dennett is arguing that HADD is useful for survival, and one of its
consequences is the propensity to be religious. I will not attempt
to settle the debate between adaptationists and non-adaptationists
here, but let me make a few observations on the implications of
the debate no matter whose side prevails.

Why Benefit?

Suppose that religiosity is natural and nearly universal because
it is directly beneficial—the adaptationist view. One thing to ask
about this proposal is how this is supposed to support atheism and
naturalism over Christianity. That is, we have been presented with
a possible explanation, a story that purports to explain religious
belief and account for the available data. But, as is often the case,
we can ask, is it the *only* explanation? Is it in fact even a *better*
explanation than that offered by a Christian understanding of
God the Creator and the human nature he has made in his own
image? If we were to make a prediction about what human nature
would be like if God made it, and if—as we read in the Westminster Catechism—the chief end of humanity is to glorify and enjoy
God forever, what would we expect to find? Would we not expect
humans to have an inward compulsion to believe in him?[16] If God
wanted us to be likely to believe and for belief to come naturally,
is it any wonder that we have the natural mechanisms for believing and that belief is beneficial? Wouldn't it be surprising if God
existed and wanted us to know him but belief were too difficult or

15. Daniel C. Dennett, *Breaking the Spell: Religion as a Natural Phenomenon* (New York: Viking, 2006), 119–20.
16. We will explore this question further in chap. 10.

harmful for most people to hold on to? As Christian philosopher Peter van Inwagen puts it:

> Suppose that God exists and wants supernaturalistic belief to be a human universal, and sees (he would see this, if it were true) that certain features that it would be useful for human beings to have—useful from an evolutionary point of view: conducive to survival and reproduction—would naturally have the consequence that supernaturalistic belief would in due course become a human universal. Why shouldn't he allow those features to be the cause of the thing he wants?—rather as the human designer of a vehicle might use the waste heat from its engine to keep its passengers warm.[17]

Suppose, on the other hand, that the non-adaptationists are right. Indeed, while this view is also not new, it does seem to be ascendant. This raises an important and significant concern. If it's true that we are so wildly misled by our faculties into believing there are ghosts or spirits or gods when really there are none, then our cognitive processes are—at least in one known instance—highly unreliable. They have massively deceived us. They have convinced the vast majority of humans throughout history that a complete fantasy is actually true.

A little later we will examine these and similar problems that arise for knowledge as we look more closely at how naturalistic evolutionary psychology undermines science, reason, and morality. But we will turn next to the neuroscience of religious experience.

---

17. Peter van Inwagen, "Explaining Belief in the Supernatural," in *The Believing Primate: Scientific, Philosophical, and Theological Reflections on the Origin of Religion*, ed. Jeffrey Schloss and Michael J. Murray (Oxford: Oxford University Press, 2009), 136.

5

Is Everything Just Brain States?

A striking feature of Christianity is the role that encounters with God have played throughout salvation history. The Bible, unlike many other repositories of religious wisdom, is not merely a collection of sages' teachings or a storehouse of spiritual insight. While it does contain those elements, it is central to the story that God has interacted with people to disclose himself—sometimes in dramatic ways and sometimes subtly. This feature is found equally in the Old and New Testaments. The authority of Scripture derives from the firm conviction that it is a reliable assemblage of testimonies recording the interactions between God and his chosen people. Indeed, if the religious experiences testified to by Moses, Isaiah, Saint Paul, and others—many, many others—had not actually taken place, the authority of the Bible would be utterly discredited.

But for someone to perceive God's presence, receive his revelations, speak his words, and follow his leading, there must be an encounter with God that is presumably mediated by the brain. Since the brain is the central organ in thinking and perceiving both external stimuli and the contents of our own minds, it must be engaged for those experiences to be had, remembered, and communicated. The question of this chapter is whether we might reasonably believe God can really be present in those and other experiences, or whether the attempts by neuroscientists to explain religious phenomena solely in terms of the brain and its activities have made it doubtful that anything transcendent is being encountered. Such attempts raise the question, are religious experiences nothing other than brain states? Is there anything veridical in our experiences of God, or do we suffer from a massive delusion foisted on us by the unique architecture of our brains?

What Is Religious Experience

A natural first question to ask is what we mean by a *religious experience* (RE).[1] To start, we can adopt the common usage in scholarly work—but we will see later that this is inadequate for a Christian understanding. The sense of RE most prevalent in cognitive science is narrower than what is usually discussed in philosophy, which in turn leaves out types of experiences discussed in theology. Because our primary concern is what cognitive science has to say about it, we will start with the narrower understanding of RE that prevails in those studies.

Just as the notion of religion is vague, so is the notion of a *religious* experience. However, in the brain science currently conducted, the focus of study has been almost exclusively on meditative practices. For variety and experimental control, participants often include practitioners of both Eastern religions (especially Buddhist monks) and Western religions (especially Catholic monks and nuns). The challenge, naturally, facing any study of such phenomena that hopes to qualify as *scientific* is that the environment and variables must be controlled, and there must lie within the practitioner some means of triggering an RE. In other words, to have a controlled environment sufficient for scientific study that will include employing a variety of brain scanning technologies,

---

1. The term itself may be somewhat unfortunate, not to mention vague, but we are stuck with it if we want to be consistent with the conversation in the literature and broader academic world.

the ideal kind of experience to study from the scientist's perspective is one that can be generated more or less at will. So one might have a methodological concern straight out of the gate. If the experiences being studied are ones that the subject knows how to create autonomously, are they really the kind of encounters with God that we usually think of? After all, if a religious experience is to be considered an encounter with God, it seems implausible to suppose that the subject can conjure one up at will, no matter how much practice he or she has had. We will return to that concern later, but for now let us look at what researchers have found.

One of the most prominent authors and researchers in the field is Andrew Newberg, a physician and neuroscience researcher who has focused his work on religion and religious experience. In his book *Why God Won't Go Away*, he describes a typical study in which a man named Robert agrees to be observed while meditating. At the "spiritual peak" of Robert's meditative practices, he reports feeling that his inner self is not an isolated entity but he is inextricably connected to all creation. Yet when he tries to put this intensely personal insight into words, he finds himself falling back on familiar clichés that have been employed for centuries to express the elusive nature of spiritual experience. "There's a sense of timelessness and infinity," he might say. "It feels like I am part of everyone and everything in existence."

Since Robert is an expert at this form of meditation and is able to induce the desired experience voluntarily, he makes an ideal candidate for investigation. He was brought into the lab, and as he began to meditate, the researchers waited for his signal. Newberg describes the scene.

> We wait one hour, while Robert meditates. Then I feel a gentle jerk on the twine. This is my cue to inject a radioactive material into a long intravenous line that also runs into Robert's room, and into a vein in his left arm. We wait a few moments more for Robert to end his meditation, then we whisk him

off to a room in the hospital's Nuclear Medicine Department, where a massive, state-of-the-art SPECT camera awaits. . . . The camera scans inside Robert's head by detecting the location of the radioactive tracer we injected when Robert tugged on the string. Because the tracer is carried by blood flow, and because this particular tracer locks almost immediately into brain cells and remains there for hours, the SPECT scans of Robert's head will give us an accurate freeze-frame of blood flow patterns in Robert's brain just moments after injection—at the high point of his meditative climax.[2]

The Investigators' Toolbox

There are several tools available to investigators. The kind Newberg used in the case of Robert is a type of CT scan, or computed tomography. Unlike some CT scans, which rely on X-rays, a SPECT (single-proton emitting computed tomography) camera is a kind of nuclear imaging that uses a radioactive dye to reveal blood flow. The more blood flow to a part of the brain, the more active it is. Another nuclear tool, a PET (positron-emission tomography) scan, operates on similar principles to track the flow of tracer elements by the blood. There are other methods as well. An MRI (magnetic resonance imaging) detects slight changes in magnetic fields caused by the electrical charges of molecules to form images. Relatedly, an fMRI (functional MRI) maps brain activity by tracking blood flow and oxygen levels to see which areas are most active. An EEG (electroencephalogram) does not produce an image but provides a squiggle chart of electrical activity in the brain. All of these tools are used in cognitive neuroscience and the investigation into religious experiences.

Most of the studies conducted on religious experience and the brain look at cases very similar to the one just described. They vary somewhat, examining the brain during private prayer, or

---

2. Andrew Newberg, Eugene D'Aquili, and Vince Rause, *Why God Won't Go Away: Brain Science and the Biology of Belief* (New York: Ballantine, 2002), 2–3.

perhaps during times of praise and worship. They scan during the reading or reciting of familiar religious texts; they evaluate neural activity during meditation. Again, methodologically these types of events lend themselves to systematic investigation. A meditating Buddhist monk who is able to put himself in a state of altered consciousness through mastery of his methods, which have been passed down for generations and honed through years of practice, can carry out his practice in laboratory conditions. Likewise, a meditating Catholic nun praying the rosary and repeatedly reciting prayers like the "Hail Mary" or "Our Father" can serve as a good subject of study, since she knows how to produce the transcendent experience. As one researcher observes:

> At present only a small number of studies exist on the relation between neural activity and religious behavior, and the majority of these have focused on how religiously inspired techniques of meditation modulate practitioners' states of consciousness. . . . Most studies have used monks, nuns or meditation experts from widely different cultures under the assumption that different forms of praying and techniques of meditation fundamentally express the same category of human experience.[3]

Indeed, overwhelmingly the literature on religious experience is flooded with studies of brains during meditation or prayer. The researchers are investigating the brain—again, in highly contrived laboratory conditions—to see how the mystical experience is played out neurologically.

Mystical Experience

Mystical experiences can be defined as experiences in which the subjects believe they encounter a supernatural being or a

---

3. Uffe Schjoedt, "The Religious Brain: A General Introduction to the Experimental Neuroscience of Religion," *Method and Theory in the Study of Religion* 21, no. 3 (2009): 310–39, quoting 311.

transcendent reality. According to the model used by Newberg, such experiences are characterized by "a breakdown in the usual sense of the passage of time; a breakdown in the usual sense of the extension of space; a breakdown in the differentiation between objects in the external world; and a breakdown in the differentiation between the self and the external world."[4] On this understanding, which has a lot more in common with Eastern philosophy than with Christianity, a mystical experience is described as a sense of union with the divine, or oneness with all things, or perhaps a dissolution of the self, as in the case of Robert above. This loss of the sense of self has been a focus of Newberg's work—a phenomenon he labels *absolute unitary being*. Here is a summary of his description of the different activities in different parts of the brain during religious experiences:

> The frontal lobes are involved in our willful behaviors. The frontal lobes are also important for what is referred to as the executive self that mediates our social behaviors, plans future events, and provides a sense of conscience and compassion. The limbic system attaches emotions to our sense of self. The temporal lobes provide a memory stream for our self and also enable us to think in abstract ways about that self. Finally the parietal lobe helps to provide a sense of space and orientation of the self. Data supports that each of these structures appears to play a role in religious and spiritual practices and experiences.

The culmination of the right combination of states in these regions of the brain gives rise to a loss of sense of individualism, according to Newberg's hypothesis. In his work studying nuns, he observed increased blood flow in the prefrontal cortex (PFC), inferior parietal lobes, and inferior frontal lobes during meditation. In Buddhist monks he studied, he found a strong positive correlation between the change of blood flow in the right PFC and the right

---

4. Newberg, D'Aquili, and Rause, *Why God Won't Go Away*, 212.

thalamus and a negative correlation with the ipsilateral superior parietal lobe.[5] Newberg summarizes, "Thus, there does seem to be an interrelationship between the brain structures that underlie the sense of self and the loss of the sense of self that is associated with many religious and spiritual experiences."[6] He claims that regardless of the *theological content* of the belief system, the neurological changes observed in the Buddhists and Catholic nuns were nearly the same.

But, Newberg rightly cautions against concluding from all of this that there is a single location, system, or activity in the brain responsible for REs, or that all REs look the same neurologically. Other parts of the brain also play an important role, including the limbic system (especially the thalamus), amygdala, and neurotransmitters and other chemicals involved in brain activity.

> To summarize, the neural varieties of religious experience are just that—varieties. There is no "God spot," nor is there any simple way to categorize religious beliefs. The data points to an endless variety of ways in which spiritual practices can affect the cognitive, emotional, and experiential processes of the brain.[7]

This is in keeping with the current understanding of the brain and how it functions. Whereas some earlier models of the brain and its regions would try to locate a specific spot where some mental phenomenon was completely sourced, contemporary researchers are eager to avoid falling into what neuroscientist and USC professor Antonio Damasio calls "the phrenological trap." In the eighteenth and early nineteenth centuries, phrenologists were pseudoscientists who thought they could analyze personality

5. Andrew Newberg, Michael Pourdehnad, Abass Alavi, and Eugene D'Aquili, "Cerebral Blood Flow during Meditative Prayer: Preliminary Findings and Methodological Issues," *Perceptual and Motor Skills* 97, no. 2 (2003): 625–30, quoting 628.

6. Andrew B. Newberg, *Principles of Neurotheology*, Ashgate Science and Religion (New York: Routledge, 2016), 152.

7. Andrew Newberg and Mark Robert Waldman, *How God Changes Your Brain: Breakthrough Findings from a Leading Neuroscientist* (New York: Ballantine, 2009), 60.

and other cognitive traits by assessing the gross anatomy of their patients, in particular by looking at bumps, depressions, and protrusions in their skulls. A bump in one region could indicate amorousness, whereas an indentation somewhere else might mean untrustworthiness. In contrast to the phrenological model, modern cognitive neuroscientists recognize that things function together as complex systems, not isolated pods. Damasio says, "To put it simply: the mind results from the operation of each of the separate components, and from the concerted operation of the multiple systems constituted by those separate components."[8] It is notoriously difficult—impossible, really—to map mental experiences precisely onto neural anatomy.

Too Much Credulity?

Keeping our focus for now only on the type of RE discussed above, Newberg and others advocate what could be called "the Executive Inhibition Hypothesis." As one team of researchers explains:

> It has been theorized that executive down-regulation in response to authoritative suggestions underpins mystical experiences. Because executive functions are supported by structural networks in frontal brain regions, the Executive Inhibition Hypothesis has been the focus of neuropsychological investigations of frontal networks, specifically the dorsolateral prefrontal cortex (dlPFC). . . . The dlPFC is involved in cognitive control, and this down-regulation has been explained in terms of a reduction of cognitive resources invested in error monitoring during religious rituals. This could lead to a tendency to believe that certain sensorial experiences we have are mystical and due to supernatural phenomena—at least partly due to inappropriate inhibitory control.[9]

---

8. Antonio Damasio, *Descartes' Error: Emotion, Reason, and the Human Brain* (New York: Quill, 1994), 15.

9. Irene Cristofori et al., "Neural Correlates of Mystical Experience," *Neuropsychologia* 80 (2016): 212–20, quoting 213.

The proposal is that mystical experience is made possible primarily in subjects who have an inadequate level of inhibition and skepticism. They are not vigilant enough at maintaining appropriate levels of doubt, instead allowing themselves to be swept away and falling prey to the power of suggestion. In fact, they share structural brain features (it is argued) with some specific types of brain damage.

> Consistent with executive theories, we found that greater mystical experience was evident in those participants with lesions in the frontal and temporal regions. These regions include the dlPFC and right superior and middle temporal cortices. . . . Patients with focal lesions to the right temporal cortex did not differ from healthy controls on the mysticism score, while patients with focal lesions in the dlPFC had substantially higher mysticism scores compared to the controls.[10]

Advocates of this hypothesis conclude that a normal, healthy brain will be better able to rein in and suppress mystical experiences because it has an intact dlPFC and therefore healthier executive function; it will be less susceptible to perverting perceptual experiences and transforming them into mystical ones. Other researchers studying lesions and religious experience have drawn similar conclusions.[11]

Other work has focused on an implication of this approach to understanding religious experience—namely, that we should be able to replicate, or at least approximate, those experiences if we can find a way to manipulate the brain into the state it enters during REs. Michael Persinger is one such researcher. He states:

> The principles [of neuroscience] indicate that all experiences, from the sense of self, to the feelings of love, to the presence

---

10. Cristofori et al., "Neural Correlates of Mystical Experience," 217.

11. See, for example, Cosimo Urgesi, Salvatore M. Aglioti, Miran Skrap, and Franco Fabbro, "The Spiritual Brain: Selective Cortical Lesions Modulate Human Self-Transcendence," *Neuron* 65, no. 3 (2010): 309–19.

of God, emerge from brain activity. If the scientist can isolate the controlling stimuli that evoke an experience, then any experience, including the experience of God, should be subject to experimental verification and reproduction within the laboratory.[12]

Persinger attracted a lot of attention in the 1990s with his development of a contraption known as the "God helmet." A modified snowmobile helmet fitted with solenoids that produce magnetic fields is placed on the subject's head, and current is run through the solenoids to create a weak magnetic field. Persinger has reported that the application of magnetic fields to the temporal lobe disrupts the person's sense of self and often leads the person to have the "absolute unitary being" experience discussed above.

In addition, subjects may experience a strong "presence" nearby that Persinger thinks corresponds to accounts of encounters with God found in sacred texts. He notes:

> We have found that stimulation of the right hemisphere by application of weak, complex magnetic fields at the level of temporoparietal lobes produced a sensed presence in about 80% of normal volunteers. Individuals with more frequent experiences classically attributed to elevated temporal lobe activity within the right hemisphere describe more elaborate and personally profound "Sentient Beings" than those only exposed to sham fields.[13]

Featured in many popular television shows and magazines, the "God helmet" has been taken by many skeptics as evidence that all purported encounters with divine beings are based in nothing but aberrant brain states that can be replicated in laboratory con-

---

12. Michael A. Persinger, "Experimental Simulation of the God Experience: Implications for Religious Beliefs and the Future of the Human Species," in *Neurotheology* (San Jose, CA: University Press, 2003), 279.

13. Michael A. Persinger, "Are Our Brains Structured to Avoid Refutations of Belief in God? An Experimental Study," *Religion* 39, no. 1 (2009): 34–42, quoting 40.

ditions.[14] If Persinger and his supporters are right, the awareness of being in God's presence reported in Scripture can be duplicated with a snowmobile helmet and some magnets.

This brings us to an important point that I have hinted at before and we may now explore in more depth. With the background studies established, we can ask the key questions: How similar are these things to encounters with God reported in Scripture? How similar are they to encounters with God reported in our era by everyday Christians? In short, do these experiments— as interesting as they may be—have any relevance to the mainstream of Christianity?

A Biblical Survey

It might be helpful to begin with cataloging biblical examples of encounters with God, or religious experiences as I have been calling them. As we will see, there are a wide variety of incidents—let us start with some of the most dramatic.

In the opening of the sixth chapter of Isaiah, the prophet reports this dramatic encounter with the living God:

> In the year that King Uzziah died I saw the Lord sitting upon a throne, high and lifted up; and the train of his robe filled the temple. Above him stood the seraphim. Each had six wings: with two he covered his face, and with two he covered his feet, and with two he flew. And one called to another and said:
>
> "Holy, holy, holy is the LORD of hosts;
> the whole earth is full of his glory!"
>
> And the foundations of the thresholds shook at the voice of him who called, and the house was filled with smoke. And I said: "Woe is me! For I am lost; for I am a man of unclean lips,

---

14. It should be noted, however, that many of Persinger's results have *not* been replicated. For example, see Roxanne Khamsi, "Electrical Brainstorms Busted as Source of Ghosts," *Nature*, December 9, 2004, https://www.nature.com/articles/news041206-10.

and I dwell in the midst of a people of unclean lips; for my eyes have seen the King, the LORD of hosts!" (vv. 1–5)

In what follows, Isaiah volunteers to bear a message from God to his people, and receives instructions from the Lord. While this book and many other prophetic books often say that the prophet received a word from the Lord (for example, after the vision is over, the very next chapter says, "And the LORD said to Isaiah," 7:3), the manner of receiving instruction and connecting with God in this episode is radical and unusual. Isaiah sees God; and not only God, but God on his throne in the heavenly temple, surrounded by worshiping heavenly creatures.

Or consider another, similar vision of God in heaven. In the opening of John's Revelation, he is "in the Spirit on the Lord's day" while in exile on the island of Patmos (Rev. 1:9–10). At first, John sees an angel who delivers him some general instructions and several specific messages to "the seven churches" (1:11). Then the scene changes. While there is a lot more detail added, his report includes this description:

> After this I looked, and behold, a door standing open in heaven! And the first voice, which I had heard speaking to me like a trumpet, said, "Come up here, and I will show you what must take place after this." At once I was in the Spirit, and behold, a throne stood in heaven, with one seated on the throne. And he who sat there had the appearance of jasper and carnelian, and around the throne was a rainbow that had the appearance of an emerald. Around the throne were twenty-four thrones, and seated on the thrones were twenty-four elders, clothed in white garments, with golden crowns on their heads. From the throne came flashes of lightning, and rumblings and peals of thunder, and before the throne were burning seven torches of fire, which are the seven spirits of God, and before the throne there was as it were a sea of glass, like crystal.

And around the throne, on each side of the throne, are four living creatures, full of eyes in front and behind: the first living creature like a lion, the second living creature like an ox, the third living creature with the face of a man, and the fourth living creature like an eagle in flight. And the four living creatures, each of them with six wings, are full of eyes all around and within, and day and night they never cease to say,

"Holy, holy, holy, is the Lord God Almighty,
who was and is and is to come!" (Rev. 4:1–8)

In another account—this one intentionally offering very little detail—the apostle Paul reports that he too had a heavenly vision. In 2 Corinthians 12 he says:

I will go on to visions and revelations of the Lord. I know a man in Christ who fourteen years ago was caught up to the third heaven—whether in the body or out of the body I do not know, God knows. And I know that this man was caught up into paradise—whether in the body or out of the body I do not know, God knows—and he heard things that cannot be told, which man may not utter. (vv. 1–4)

The book of Acts records how Stephen, the first martyr of the church, had the following experience while he was being stoned for his testimony about Jesus Christ: "But [Stephen], full of the Holy Spirit, gazed into heaven and saw the glory of God, and Jesus standing at the right hand of God. And he said, 'Behold, I see the heavens opened, and the Son of Man standing at the right hand of God'" (Acts 7:55–56).

These accounts are obviously very different from what has been studied and reported on by neuroscientists, and clearly could not be produced on demand to satisfy the curiosity of researchers in a lab. While many other such encounters are recorded in the Bible, the ones quoted here are good representatives of the kind of transported vision that often reveals important things about God through the Scriptures. If they play an important role in salvation history and in Christian knowledge, it is not by being the kind of REs that neuroscientists have done anything at all to illuminate. Their work is utterly irrelevant.

But admittedly not all REs or encounters with God in the Bible are this dramatic either. Without involving a vision of God in heaven, they nevertheless represent divine encounters and the revelation of knowledge. One such additional important way God discloses himself and his will is through dreams. In the first two chapters of Matthew's Gospel alone, God connects with people and discloses himself and his will several times through dreams. While Joseph was considering divorcing Mary for being pregnant, an angel appeared to him and told him to marry her (1:20). After presenting gifts to the newborn Jesus, the wise men were warned in a dream not to return to Herod (2:12). Joseph was told in a dream to move his family to Egypt (2:13), and then in another dream to return to Israel (2:19–20)—but, in another dream, to move somewhere besides Judea (2:22). Even today, there are many stories of God revealing the way of salvation through faith in Jesus Christ to Muslims through dreams—Muslims who had no knowledge of Jesus but were later taught the gospel by missionaries for whom they had been prepared by the dream encounters.[15]

Dreams and Visions

Though dreams have received less attention than the studies of meditation and religious experience discussed so far, apart from their religious context dreams have also been the subject of extensive brain study. Not surprisingly, many neuroscientists think their work has shown that these are not encounters with God at all but nothing more than indigestion of the skull. Skeptics dismiss any

15. For examples, see Tom Doyle, *Dreams and Visions: Is Jesus Awakening the Muslim World?* (Nashville: Thomas Nelson, 2012); Nabeel Qureshi, *Seeking Allah, Finding Jesus: A Devout Muslim Encounters Christianity* (Grand Rapids, MI: Zondervan, 2018); Jerry Trousdale, *Miraculous Movements: How Hundreds of Thousands of Muslims Are Falling in Love with Jesus* (Nashville: Thomas Nelson, 2012).

supernatural element by chalking it all up to random brain activity during the REM (rapid eye movement) stage of sleep. Reports growing out of one seminal dream study document that

> subjects in the sleep laboratory who were awakened during a stage of REM sleep were much more likely to report a dream than people awakened during a state of NREM sleep, and the REM dream reports frequently involved "strikingly vivid visual imagery," suggesting that "it is indeed highly probable that rapid eye movements are directly associated with visual imagery in dreaming."[16]

These might seem like encounters with God to those having them, but the skeptic says they are nothing other than the natural result of "adaptive functions that . . . include storing memories and newly learned skills, processing information with a high emotional charge, responding to waking-life crises, making wide-range connections in the mind, and practicing adaptive types of behavior."[17] Our brains emit dreams like our metabolic processes emit heat—they are just the by-products of the processing of inputs to each system.

In fact, some brain researchers claim that dreams and visions share the same neural patterns of activity. If one were to examine brain scans without knowing independently whether the subject was awake or asleep when the scans were taken, we could not tell from the scans alone, some suggest. That is, without additional information the EEG would not be able to distinguish between a sleeper's dream and a vision (or, a skeptic would say, a *delusion*) of someone awake. The brain ends up in a similar state either way. The explanation from a neuroscience perspective says, "Much of this heightened neural activity can be attributed to the phasic discharge of ponto-geniculo-occipital (PGO) waves originating in the

---

16. Kelly Bulkeley, *The Wondering Brain: Thinking about Religion with and beyond Cognitive Neuroscience* (New York: Routledge, 2005), 31.
17. Bulkeley, *The Wondering Brain*, 31.

brainstem and spreading throughout the cortical and subcortical regions of the brain."[18]

What are we to conclude about the reports in the Bible of people encountering God through visions and dreams? The first thing to note is that the visions and dreams we just surveyed bear little or no resemblance to the REs studied by neuroscientists. In fact, it seems difficult to imagine the biblical characters agreeing to subject themselves to study on the basis of the experiences they reported having. They would likely insist that these encounters were with the living God and totally the result of God's initiative, and nothing they could do would be able to generate something similar for the scientists to study. They did not produce these experiences themselves by mastering mystical techniques. And they would have had enough practical experience with living life that they could distinguish between regular dreams and encounters with God—they would not have assumed that every dream carried a secret divine message. Everyone knows sometimes a dream is just a dream.

Second, regardless of whether scientists can generate a model of the brain states of dreams and visions, it simply would not follow that those experiences were not of God. After all, my brain is in a certain state when I perceive, say, a giraffe. If careful enough brain mapping could locate just which parts of the brain were activated by giraffe perceptions, would that mean that we no longer had grounds for believing in giraffes? That giraffe experiences were nothing but brain states with no connection to an external reality? What if we could manipulate a subject's brain to replicate a giraffe experience in the laboratory—would *that* mean there are no giraffes in reality? That conclusion would be laughable from the evidence available. Cambridge-trained brain scientist Dr. Sharon Dirckx puts it well:

> Should Christians be fearful that neuroscience is squeezing God out of the picture? Not at all. Just because something is

18. Bulkeley, *The Wondering Brain*, 32.

experienced through the brain, that does not necessarily mean it *originated in* the brain. . . . And if God *does* exist, then it comes as no surprise that he would make us such that our brains are active when we encounter him. This kind of data is not a threat to religious, and specifically Christian, belief. Of course, if you believe that we are our brains, then one could argue that brain activity explains away religious experience. But if there is a distinct mind that influences the brain, then brain activity is only one of several different types of explanation. To conclude that we must choose between activity in the brain and the reality of God is to sell ourselves short. Both are needed to fully understand religious experience. . . .

The God revealed in the pages of the Bible has made people with both physical and spiritual dimensions. A person is a mysterious and beautiful embodiment of both the physical and the spiritual working together. If encounters with God are real, we would expect them to engage the brain rather than bypass it. Brain activity, far from being a threat to God, is exactly what we would predict.[19]

It seems, then, that the much-vaunted findings of neuroscience are either irrelevant or comfortably compatible with Christianity. We were promised explanations—or even refutations—of Christian belief, and instead we were presented with findings that have not discredited the witness of the Bible in the least.

"Ordinary" Religious Experiences

There are other ways in which the research findings have missed the mark as well. By focusing almost exclusively on self-induced mystical experiences, they have neglected the kind of religious encounters most common to the life of ordinary believers, and of ultimately far more importance. The Bible reports a lot of ways we encounter and are affected by God. Most Christians have not

---

19. Sharon Dirckx, *Am I Just My Brain?* (n.p.: Good Book, 2019), 112–13.

seen a vision like Isaiah's, heard the audible voice of God, or received instructions from angels through a dream. Even those who report such experiences would admit they are rare. But apart from those, the Bible teaches us about many other, less dramatic ways God reveals himself and interacts with us. Consider the following verses, a very small sample of what we could refer to:

- "And when [the Holy Spirit] comes, he will convict the world concerning sin and righteousness and judgment" (John 16:8).
- "When the Spirit of truth comes, he will guide you into all the truth, for he will not speak on his own authority" (John 16:13).
- "When they deliver you over, do not be anxious how you are to speak or what you are to say, for what you are to say will be given to you in that hour" (Matt. 10:19).
- "The Spirit himself bears witness with our spirit that we are children of God" (Rom. 8:16).
- "I write these things to you about those who are trying to deceive you. But the anointing that you received from him abides in you, and you have no need that anyone should teach you. But as his anointing teaches you about everything, and is true, and is no lie—just as it has taught you, abide in him" (1 John 2:26–27).
- "And we know that the Son of God has come and has given us understanding, so that we may know him who is true; and we are in him who is true, in his Son Jesus Christ. He is the true God and eternal life" (1 John 5:20).

These kinds of religious experiences are normative in the life of the Christian, not the dramatic dreams and visions. These often quiet, even unnoticed activities of God are what characterize our lives after the new birth in Jesus Christ. We will discuss in a later chapter the rationality of treating these as a foundation for knowledge, but for now we can note that these fit the meaning of religious experiences: they are clearly presented by the biblical authors as encounters with God. In these things we have contact with the divine, and it transforms us. The transformation is slow, but the process of being progressively brought into conformity with the image of Christ and bearing the fruit of the Holy Spirit is always treated in Scripture as the work of God in us—not something we manufacture ourselves but something in which God, the divine physician, acts upon us, his patients. This slow, steady work of God is the real kind of religious experience that matters in everyday Christianity. As philosopher Elton Trueblood comments:

> Ordinarily religious experience has nothing to do with visions, ecstasies, raptures or other phenomena which are usually considered abnormal. It is true that some mystics have experienced these exalted states of consciousness or unconsciousness, but they are no part of *normative* religious experience. On the contrary, such experience is as unspectacular as breathing or sleeping. For most men and women, religious experience has been a calm assurance of the reality of a relationship which gives meaning to existence.[20]

The Bible and Christian theologians throughout history have taught that we experience God in all these ways and more. When we feel the weight of conviction for sin, that is a religious experience because it is God interacting with us by his Spirit. When we feel moved to pray for someone or moved to praise God for his goodness and mercy, those things are initiated by God himself as we walk with him. Those too are religious experiences—encounters with God that affect us by, among other things, affecting our brains. When the claims of Scripture ring true to us and they come to mind when we need insight and instruction, those are religious experiences too. All of these are times when what we think, feel, and do—which undoubtedly involve our brains—is because God is touching us. None of them is really captured or addressed by

---

20. Elton Trueblood, *Philosophy of Religion* (Grand Rapids, MI: Baker, 1983), 148.

any of the brain science studies of religious experience, but they are the bread and butter of daily Christian living. In the final analysis, then, there is very little in the highly publicized studies of brains and REs that is relevant to Christianity, and none of it in any way destroys, or even diminishes, the credibility of the Bible's testimony that we can and do interact with God himself.

6

Doing Away with the Soul

As we look around and see all the kinds of living things that surround us—dogs and cats, fish and fowl, bats and bugs, and countless other critters—we find an astonishing array of forms of life. Nearly every nook and cranny of our planet teems with life, and even the most uninhabitable places host some kind of organism. They range from enormous blue whales to microscopic bacteria. Buried underground is an assortment of now-extinct creatures like dinosaurs, things previously thought to exist only in the imagination. With all of these living things we can feel a connection, and we hold features in common. We all take in nourishment and grow, each in its own way. All life needs water and ultimately depends on sunlight. We all have DNA and RNA. All organisms require oxygen and carbon, the building blocks of life. We all reproduce and have offspring: trees and turtles and trilobites alike. Many other animals even play, enjoy naps in the sun, and form social groups. Especially with the higher animals, we feel kinship and even affection. We genuinely love our pets and have a connection with them that we would never have with a stone or any other inanimate object. The relationship my son has with our dog really is a kind of friendship.

Similar–but Different

Even so, there is a troubling trend to downplay our vast differences from other organisms in order to emphasize our similarities.
The failure to adequately appreciate the gulf that distinguishes
human nature from that of the beasts has led to the denigration
of human nature—a dethroning of the divine image bearers. The
prevailing perspective is that humans, rather than being "a little
lower than the heavenly beings" (Ps. 8:5), are merely a little
higher than the great apes. But despite our similarity to all other
living things, we must recognize that there is something fundamentally different about humans; we are not merely another animal. Even the great apes on their best day cannot hold a candle
to human beings.

Attempts to ignore those differences by appealing, for example, to the structure of our brains or the similarity of our
DNA tell a very misleading story. It may be true that we share
something like 97 percent of our DNA with chimps,[1] but the
vast differences between us make that number seem irrelevant.
Granted, we have many genetic features and even behaviors in
common, but why should DNA be the main determiner of our
likeness? DNA is one kind of similarity, but it is not the only
ground for drawing comparisons.

Likewise, it is undeniable that our brain structure shows amazing similarities to that of other primates. But can looking closely at
those similarities obscure our uniqueness? In one paper describing
human brains as merely "the extreme of a lateralized ape trend,"
the scientists describe their work like this:

> Comparative investigations of the prefrontal cortex may thus
> shed more light on the neural underpinnings of what makes
> us human. Using histological data from 19 anthropoid pri-
> mate species (6 apes including humans and 13 monkeys),

---

1. This number is controversial and has prompted a lot of critical discussion. Even so, we
can employ it here simply for its popularity in the public consciousness.

we investigate cross-species relative size changes along the anterior (prefrontal) and posterior (motor) axes of the cyto-architectonically defined frontal lobe in both hemispheres. [We] suggest that the primary factor underlying the evolution of primate brain architecture is left hemispheric prefrontal hyperscaling, and indicate that humans are the extreme of a left prefrontal ape specialization in relative white to gray matter volume.[2]

There is no need to question the findings of this research. The brains it studied probably do show those distinctions. However, regardless of its scientific accuracy, there is a philosophical concern here: the impression left by work like this is that humans differ from other primates only as a matter of degree, not in kind. Is that a satisfying perspective, or does it seem to miss something?

When we look past the resemblances that scientists emphasize and reflect on the differences, we see that we are worlds apart regardless of genetic and brain similarities. How does chimpanzee romantic poetry compare with ours? Or philosophy? Or any kind of art or science or engineering? When chimps tell stories—whether orally, through books, or through movies—are they nearly as funny or moving as ours? When they worship God, do they use similar musical instruments or worship in similar buildings or read from similar Scriptures? When they plant and plow fields and ship crops across land and sea, is their machinery almost as durable and efficient as ours? It is said that they use tools because they may poke a stick in a tree stump to fish out the ants. Does that use of tools really compare to the Mars Rovers?

This is all facetious, of course. Chimps and orangutans and gorillas don't just fail to do those things as well as we do; they don't do them at all. In focusing on the similarities, we can easily forget just how deep and wide is the chasm that separates us from

2. J. B. Smaers et al., "Primate Prefrontal Cortex Evolution: Human Brains Are the Extreme of a Lateralized Ape Trend," *Brain, Behavior, and Evolution* 77, no. 2 (2011): 67.

them. Traditionally, this human uniqueness has been understood in terms of a soul—something humans have that nothing else does.

The Progress of Science

When I was a sophomore in college, I took Introduction to Psychology. It was an interesting class, especially as a counterbalance to all the physics, math, and chemistry I was taking. My professor, no friend of religion, gave us a history of the field that went something like this: "Back in the bad old days, when people were stupid, they didn't understand anything and thought everything was the fault of gods and spirits. They thought lightning was a sign of divine anger, as were earthquakes, floods, drought, volcanoes, forest fires, and just about every other calamity. On the other hand, they thought good crops, peace, and prosperity were sure signs of divine blessing. Now, however, we understand that those things are all the results of natural causes. Lightning isn't a sign of divine anger; it's a sign that there's a buildup of too many electrons in a cloud, and they generate enough electric potential to jump to earth. Drought might be from an ongoing El Niño event. Earthquakes are from the shifting of tectonic plates, and so on. In the same way, our unenlightened forebears thought that what animated a person was a soul—some kind of spirit living in your body, pulling the strings like a puppeteer. But now we understand it's all just a matter of brain states and there is nothing more to it than that. It's a very complicated story, to be sure, but it's ultimately and exclusively a *physical* story—a story about matter in motion. There is no soul inside your body; there is only your body."

This is a common narrative, and psychology and neuroscience have grown and flourished in the soil of metaphysical materialism. Consider this a version of what we can call the "progress of science" argument, or PSA. Roughly speaking, PSA says that the idea of an immaterial, spiritual nature was concocted to explain the complex nature of thought and consciousness. It was plausible at one time to believe that people were a mix of body and soul, but the progress of science has left no room for anything but the physical. The claim, in short, is that we no longer need souls. There is nothing for them to do. For instance, consider this statement:

> In other words, science explains these features of consciousness without invoking a non-physical soul. So there is, at least with respect to all of these aspects of conscious experience, no explanatory work for a non-physical soul to do. The steady march of progress and explanatory successes already achieved in neuroscience and its cognate disciplines, coupled with the *continued* progress and successes we can expect in the future, leaves less and less room for a non-physical soul. The ongoing success of the neurosciences is squeezing the soul out of the explanatory picture.[3]

With the growth in understanding of the brain and how it functions, contempt for the older dualist accounts has grown. In basic outline, the progress argument looks at the dualistic account as a soul-of-the-gaps substitute for real understanding; it is merely folk psychology masquerading as insight. The reason people believe in souls, the progressivists state, is very similar to the reason people believed in tree spirits and volcano goddesses: they needed an explanation and didn't know where else to turn. Psychologist Malcolm Jeeves states it this way: "Some [dualists] take a 'soul-of-the-gaps' position, much like the older 'god-of-the-gaps position,' using the concept of the 'soul' to explain those human experiences that we cannot (yet, at least) explain neurologically or biologically."[4] Just as science has moved gods and ancestors and

---

3. Kevin Corcoran and Kevin Sharpe, "Neuroscience and the Human Person," in *Neuroscience and the Soul: The Human Person in Philosophy, Science, and Theology*, ed. Thomas M. Crisp, Steven L. Porter, and Gregg A. Ten Elshof (Grand Rapids, MI: Eerdmans, 2016), 130.
4. Malcolm Jeeves, "Toward a Composite Portrait of Human Nature," in *From Cells to Souls—and Beyond: Changing Portraits of Human Nature*, ed. Malcom Jeeves (Grand Rapids, MI: Eerdmans, 2004), 245.

other spirits out of our explanations of natural events, the PSA insists that science has left no work for souls to do and no reason to believe in them.

No More Souls

In the twentieth century it became common, especially for behavioral psychologists but also for physicalists of many other stripes, to use disparaging terms like "ghost" to refer to the soul or spirit. As one particularly aggressive anti-dualist philosopher named Gilbert Ryle put it, when discussing dualism in any form, "I shall often speak of it, with deliberate abusiveness, as 'the dogma of the Ghost in the Machine.'"[5]

The way Ryle describes it, Galileo and Descartes (and later, but crucially, Newton) had demonstrated clearly that their methods of science were sufficient to explain the behaviors of nearly every kind of object in nature. And if humans are mere objects in nature, then everything about the behavior of our bodies—including our brains, and therefore (if you're a materialist) everything we say and do—should also be explicable in those same mechanical terms. But, says Ryle:

> Descartes found in himself two conflicting motives. As a man of scientific genius he could not but endorse the claims of mechanics, yet as a religious and moral man he could not accept . . . that human nature differs only in degree of complexity from clockwork. The mental could not just be a variety of the mechanical.[6]

Ryle thought it was Descartes's old-fashioned, prescientific religious thinking that held him back and motivated him to believe that there is a "ghost in the machine" despite what the progress of science had clearly demonstrated. PSA says that a (forgivable) ignorance of the underlying forces that control all matter gave rise

---

5. Gilbert Ryle, *The Concept of Mind* (Chicago: University of Chicago Press, 2000), 15.
6. Ryle, *The Concept of Mind*, 19.

to belief in the immaterial aspect of human persons; but the refusal or inability to come to grips with the new physicalist, mechanistic program explained the ongoing acceptance of dualism. But now, say Ryle and others, these antiquated views must go. They are no longer credible in the modern age.[7]

When a view is seen as old-fashioned, it is often rejected as being unscientific. This argumentative tactic can be found as far back as 400 BC among the Greeks. The way the brain science culture winds are blowing now, if someone thinks that the fundamental problems of consciousness and human constitution are still not solved to our satisfaction, and that all the findings of modern research are consistent with mind-body dualism, that person is characterized as a science denier. Thus, psychologist Daniel Robinson observes:

> It is not uncommon for the modern behaviorist or physiological psychologist to express disbelief when scholars entertaining other perspectives insist that a scientific account of human action and human experience is not any nearer than it was in pre-Socratic times. There is, mixed with this disbelief, a conviction often stated that those who do not subscribe to the behavioristic or physiological accounts are clutching at the straws of metaphysical dualism and religious mysticism. It seems that this reaction to the scholar's reservation is prompted by the view that such a reservation must be based on a denial of science's role in psychological studies. That is, to reject the behaviorist or physiological accounts is somehow, *ipso facto*, tantamount to rejecting science itself.[8]

---

7. Ryle compares belief in something immaterial above and beyond the body to believing that "team spirit" refers to a special kind of immaterial entity above and beyond all the players of a team. If a baseball team (or, in Ryle's example, a cricket team) has team spirit, there is still nothing beyond the players of the team. There is no additional immaterial substance or soul or ghost that unifies and transcends the team. Instead, "team spirit" is just an expression we use when the members of the team cooperate well and have affection for one another.

8. Daniel N. Robinson, *An Intellectual History of Psychology* (Madison: University of Wisconsin Press, 1986), 453–54.

While that approach is popular, it does not stand up under scrutiny. The reasons people have for believing in souls are myriad, but there is little or no support for the claim that soul-of-the-gaps reasoning is at the heart of it. Some may believe in souls for that reason, but the claim that they do is generally made without any evidence that they arrive at their conviction as an ad hoc solution to an explanatory puzzle. Just as it is unlikely that most people believe in God in order to explain mysterious natural occurrences, it is equally unlikely that most people believe in souls in order to explain mysterious mental occurrences. Says one philosopher about this accusation:

> Indeed, the view seems to be thoroughly groundless. Without question, those in the Plato—Augustine—Descartes line (which includes Butler and Reid) believe in the soul's existence on the basis of what they are aware of from the first-person perspective. There is not the least bit of evidence for the idea that they arrive at their belief in the soul's existence after failing to explain various experiences in terms of what goes on in the physical world.[9]

Surely people believe in souls for a variety of reasons—but it is doubtful that their arguments are as weak and lazy as the gap accusation implies. In fact, despite this modern dismissive attitude (what C. S. Lewis called "chronological snobbery"), people have thought long and hard about souls and done so with pretty extensive and impressive knowledge of the mind-body connection. A little history here, for context, might help.

A History of Souls

Greek philosophy, an important source for all Western thought, frequently featured discussions of the soul. Some Greeks were materialists and atomists, just like our materialists today; they

---

9. Stewart Goetz and Charles Taliaferro, "The Soul and Contemporary Science," in *A Brief History of the Soul* (Chichester: John Wiley, 2011), 154–55.

even used many of the same arguments to support their view that everything is material. Others, however, were staunch defenders of dualism and immaterial realities of all kinds. The use of the term for "soul" in classical Greek can sometimes be confusing, having multiple senses that apply to other things than humans. In the works of Plato, for instance, the term we translate as "soul" had a wide application that went beyond the way we usually use the word now. All living things were thought to possess some type of soul. Anything that is capable of moving itself, whether through locomotion or even through growth, has a sort of "soul."[10]

Even so, beyond what everything else has (viz. the power to grow and move and take in nourishment), humans were considered to have something different: the *rational* soul. This soul belongs *only* to humans and is what distinguishes us from all other forms of life. To Plato and many other Greek philosophers, the rational soul—or what we would normally now just call the soul, for simplicity—was considered a separate immaterial component to a person that was not identical to the body and could survive the body's death. The rational soul, the part unique to humans, was different in kind from the other types of souls shared by other living things. This rational soul was spiritual, and Plato believed it existed before it was joined to a body and would continue to exist after parting ways with the body. So those who would be wise, said Plato, should strive to bring about "the parting of the soul from the body . . . away from every part of the body . . . in the hereafter, released from the body, as from fetters."[11]

When we move about two thousand years forward to the early modern period of the seventeenth and eighteenth centuries, we still see that dualistic mind-body view dominating the scholarly world. For example, René Descartes, a seventeenth-century French philosopher, is famous for his arguments that soul and body are

---

10. We can see parallels of that sentiment in the Old Testament use of the Hebrew words *nephesh* and *ruach* for "soul," "spirit," or "life principle," not only in reference to humans but also for everything that has the breath of life.

11. *Phaedo* 67c–d.

distinct. Like Plato, Descartes believed that soul and body were of different natures—one material, one immaterial. And Descartes was also aware of the close connection between mind and brain, but this did not deter him from dualism. He said:

> Now I maintain that when God unites a rational soul to this machine [meaning the body] . . . he will place its principal seat in the brain, and will make its nature such that the soul will have different sensations corresponding to the different ways in which the entrances to the pores in the internal surface of the brain are opened by means of the nerves.[12]

Affirming the clear distinction between body and soul, he nevertheless rejected what he saw as the sharp separation of soul and body found in Plato, arguing that "I am not merely present in my body as a sailor is present in a ship, but that I am very closely joined and, as it were, intermingled with it, so that I and the body form a unit." He also spoke of the "union and, as it were, intermingling of the mind with the body."[13] He was in the vanguard of understanding the role of the brain in thinking, yet still accepted the basic dualistic framework.

This was not only the view of academics but also the view of everyday people. Even today, the findings of social science researchers indicate that belief in souls is overwhelmingly common in America and throughout the world. As one team of authors has noted:

> Belief in the Soul Hypothesis [is not] merely a quirk of the Western intellectual tradition. If it were, it could perhaps be blamed on the idiosyncratic influence of some charismatic but slightly whacky figure, a Plato or a St. Paul. But on the

---

12. René Descartes, *The Philosophical Writings of Descartes*, trans. John Cottingham, Robert Stoothoff, and Dugald Murdoch, vol. 1 (Cambridge: Cambridge University Press, 1999), 102.

13. René Descartes, *The Philosophical Writings of Descartes*, trans. John Cottingham, Robert Stoothoff, and Dugald Murdoch, vol. 2 (Cambridge: Cambridge University Press, 1999), 56.

contrary, it is a long-standing result of cultural anthropology that such a belief is attested in almost all known human cultures. In a classic study in the anthropology of religious belief, Sir Edward Burnett Tylor—one of the founding figures of scientific anthropology—identified "the doctrine of souls" as a basic belief underlying social and religious practices in all "primitive" human societies. . . . More recent anthropologists interested in universal features of human culture have agreed with this classic assessment.[14]

In addition, cognitive science research has shown clearly that children manifest a tendency to believe in the soul hypothesis and a propensity to categorize mental and physical events as fundamentally different. It seems that belief in souls truly is nearly universal and natural. The noteworthy exception is the small segment of contemporary Western intellectuals who reject it.

Objections to Souls

That nearly universal tendency, of course, is no proof of anything, but it is suggestive—the belief that we are not merely material objects dominates history as well as the contemporary world. But since belief in souls is under such attack in the West, especially in academia, we will turn now to a set of arguments by modern physicalists *against* the existence of immaterial souls to see if their arguments are as compelling as they are touted to be. As I promised earlier, we will later consider some arguments that try to show the inadequacy of physicalist views of human nature, but for now I will focus on responding to the arguments against dualism.

Proponents of PSA do not usually insist that those who continue to believe in souls are irrational. They recognize that science does not *prove* there are no souls. It is only the most strident who make extravagant claims of proof. Those who are more charitable

---

14. Mark C. Baker and Stewart Goetz, *The Soul Hypothesis: Investigations into the Existence of the Soul* (New York: Bloomsbury Academic, 2011), 2–3.

argue instead that there is no explanatory role for the immaterial, and the progress of science has rationally undercut any reason for believing in it.

Those who doubt the existence of souls generally depend upon a common objection. In their minds, the issue of parsimony in ontology and explanation is primary. That is, generally speaking we want to follow the advice of Ockham's razor and avoid "multiplying entities beyond necessity." If the explanatory work we have to do can be done by physical stuff only, then—all other things being equal—we should avoid adding any extra entities into the mix. Metaphysician Nikk Effingham espouses this principle when he says,

> Because an explanation in merely material terms is sufficient for what goes on in the world (that is, physicalism seems to do the trick when it comes to explaining our mental lives), we should naturally favor the theory with just one kind of substance, i.e., discard substance dualism in favor of some physicalist theory about the mind.[15]

A soul, progressivists say, is an explanatorily useless appendage; it is excess ontological baggage better left at the bus station.[16]

It seems to me that part of what gives rise to this view is thinking that the materialist accounts of human nature and our mental lives are more successful than they really are. Granted, they are ontologically streamlined in virtue of having jettisoned souls and kept only brains, but it does not seem that they have actually been able to say how the brain gives rise to the richness of experience that has traditionally been attributed to the activity of the soul. How does that lump of gray and white matter *do*

---

15. Nikk Effingham, *An Introduction to Ontology* (Cambridge: Polity, 2013), 39.

16. Note that no one seems to want to take Ockham's razor to its logical limits. If we did, we would all end up as solipsists, people who believe that only they exist and everything else is merely an aspect of their own minds. That thesis can be made to fit with all our experiences and all the available data, and it has the most ontological parsimony possible—the existence of just one single thing. The razor is only of relative and limited value.

that? Have the materialists really cracked that nut, or are they exaggerating their success?

The "Hard Problem"

Perhaps one of the most effective critics along these lines is Australian philosopher David Chalmers. He distinguishes between the "easy problems" and the "hard problem" of consciousness. The easy problems, he says, are the ones surrounding the structure and operations of the brain and central nervous system. This is the stuff of brain studies, and our knowledge of those structures has increased rapidly and is now astounding. However, as Chalmers explains, even exhaustive knowledge of those structures will not explain the nature of consciousness itself. There is a *feel* to conscious experience. There is something *it is like* to be in pain, or to daydream, or to feel happy. Many philosophers and scientists believe that explaining everything involved in thinking *at the level of the brain* will automatically mean explaining *everything there is* to our mental and spiritual life. But Chalmers is unconvinced. He says:

> Physical explanation is well suited to the explanation of structure and function. . . . But the explanation of consciousness is not just a matter of explaining structure and function. Once we have explained all the physical structure in the vicinity of the brain, and we have explained how all the various brain functions are performed, there is a further sort of explanandum: consciousness itself. Why should all this structure and function give rise to experience? The story about the physical process does not say.[17]

The problem of connecting mechanisms to mental life has at least two aspects. The first is the point Chalmers is making, that understanding all the physical structures underlying our mental

17. David J. Chalmers, *The Conscious Mind: In Search of a Fundamental Theory* (Oxford: Oxford University Press, 1996), 107.

life (assuming they do so) does not in any way explain the connection between those structures and the thoughts themselves. A thought is not like a collection of neurons. Pain is not like C-fibers firing. The mechanisms do not really do anything to explain the phenomena of conscious experience. Why should an arrangement of physical stuff like that create consciousness? Nothing in our understanding of the nature of matter or the constitution of our brains gives even the slightest hint at an explanation. At the end of the story, all a materialist has to say is, "Well . . . it just *does*." It would not be predicted from even the most comprehensive understanding of the structures and mechanisms of the brain.

In fact, there is something suspicious about the whole enterprise of trying to reduce and explain the entirety of our mental lives in terms of chemical and physical processes. The hard problem focuses on the difficulty of such accounts and the slim prospects of bridging the explanatory gap between mental and physical. That is:

> The task, in other words, should not lie with trying to fit the mental into the physical, but how to understand the physical in relationship to the mental. Arguably, the neuroscientist does not just have hints that she is thinking, feeling awe, and is engaged in neuroscience; she should be certain of this, and if she does not observe the thinking, feeling awe, and the active practice of neuroscience in the observable, "unambiguously chemical or electrical" brain events or any other "thoroughly physical" phenomena, that is good reason for her to believe that thinking, feeling awe, and so on are not identical with such physical events and phenomena.[18]

There is still simply no adequate scientific model linking the mental and physical, or explaining the emergence of the mental from

---

18. Charles Taliaferro, "The Promise and Sensibility of Integrative Dualism," in *Contemporary Dualism: A Defense*, ed. Andrea Lavazza and Howard Robinson (New York: Routledge, 2014), 201–2.

the physical. Despite the correlations that everyone is fully aware of and always has been, this is an embarrassing and troubling lacuna. In the words of Christian philosopher Kelly James Clark:

> After years of thought and effort, we still have no idea how the painful ache in our knees, the perception of the redness of a rose, or the sweet taste of honey arises from the brain chemicals or neural processes that are correlated with those conscious thoughts or feelings. . . . How do things with entirely physical properties cause or give rise to things with entirely mental properties? What is the relationship of the mental to the physical? We simply don't know.[19]

But if the explanation is still so far from complete (or maybe hasn't even been started), what is left of the argument against souls? Many scientists boast that they have solved the problem of consciousness by explaining all the mechanisms of the brain. We have seen that this is a false boast. But if there is a seriously *hard* problem that is not yet solved (and that seems to be the case), then furthermore it cannot be true that science has eliminated the soul.

Why not? Because eliminating the soul *depends* on solving the problem of consciousness as a necessary first step. The allegation is that we should no longer believe in souls because science has solved the problem of consciousness, leaving nothing for souls to do. As we indicated already, the soul-of-the-gaps argument is not why most people believe in souls, but even if it were, the failure to solve the hard problem means that consciousness has not actually been explained anyway. There could still be just as much explanatory work for the soul to do now as in Plato's day. Despite all the progress in understanding the brain, its structure, and its functions, some things still elude explanation—the hard problem remains just as hard as ever.

---

19. Kelly James Clark, *God and the Brain: A Rationality of Belief* (Grand Rapids, MI: Eerdmans, 2019), 19.

Why Believe Something Exists?

Another problem lurks nearby. It is a more philosophical concern, but there may be an underlying presupposition about existence claims that needs to be thought through. In short, do we have reason for believing in the existence of something only if its existence is necessary for scientific explanation? That is, do we have the right to believe an entity exists only if we need it to do science? The unstated line of reasoning could be put succinctly this way: we do not need to assume a person is anything other than a body to do our best science, so there is no good reason to believe a person is anything other than a body.

We've just seen one problem with this kind of argument: the difficulty of living up to the extravagant promise to be able to explain our mental lives just by reference to mechanisms. But the other problem is that it is hard to see why the needs of science—and the needs of science *alone*—get to arbitrate our beliefs in this way. This prejudice closes the door on the possibility that we might have justified reasons for believing in the existence of something, even though the object in question (in this case, souls) has no scientific work to do. When we state it clearly, the premise is that *the only possible good reasons for believing in something must be scientific.*

But why should we think that? Why should we rule out, as a stipulation from the beginning, having good but nonscientific reasons for our beliefs—reasons like, for example, experience, memory, intuition, testimony, logical inference, or even divine design or divine revelation? I cannot see why we should share this prejudice, and I have never seen a convincing argument in defense of it. It is certainly not something science has concluded, nor could it be. Science could never show us that only science can determine existence claims. But if it is *false* that only science can determine existence claims—or even *possibly* false—then what is *true*, or at least *possibly* true, is that there can be nonscientific, justifiable reasons for believing in something even if it has no scientific utility whatsoever.

The upshot is that it's not terribly relevant whether science has any use for souls. We can grant that the usefulness science has for an entity, or the extent to which scientists offer explanations of some entity's nature, is sometimes important. Homunculi, phlogiston, caloric, the ether—these obsolete scientific notions have all been abandoned because they served no scientific purpose and mapped onto no observable objects. We need not question that it was (probably) right to discard them.[20] But it is equally mistaken to conclude that every entity science does not need is therefore mythical. And again, that assumes something that has not really been shown anyway, that science has no need of the immaterial. Scientific usefulness is not the only criterion for determining whether belief in something is justified.

Spirit and Matter Interact

The last problem we will consider in this chapter is related to a misrepresentation of Christian thought we explored earlier—namely, the false dichotomy in pitting *what happens naturally* against *what God does*. In the same vein as that discussion, we can ask here why we must put the activity of the soul in tension with the activity of the brain instead of viewing them as cooperating causes—two aspects of a complete understanding of human nature. Why insist that *what the brain does* could not overlap with *what the soul does*?

We saw earlier, especially with the models of divine action known as concurrentism and occasionalism, that those were attempts to understand how *what God does* is related to *what happens in nature*. Each of those models makes it consistent to say—as the biblical authors insisted on—that events occurring in nature are also acts of God, even when those events follow natural laws and arise in the "normal" course of events. That is, salt does not dissolve in water apart from divine action. When we study and

---

20. Though, for the record, I'm not convinced there is no ether.

reveal the underlying patterns of nature, there are neither theologi- cal nor scientific reasons to suppose that we have removed God from the picture. All events in the natural world are the outwork- ing of God's purposes, done according to his plans and brought into reality by his power.

The lesson from looking at the models of divine action is that God acting in the world, by any of the models, is completely consistent with the world operating according to laws of nature. Against the common prejudice, there is no conflict in saying both *this is how God acts* and *this is how nature operates*. In the same way, there need be no conflict in saying both that our brains and physical structures are operating at the root of our mental lives and that our souls are. (And for that matter, that God is too.) Again, even supposing that mechanical, chemical, physical, bio- logical descriptions of the causes of our mental states are possible, that would still not be incompatible with spiritual causes being in operation too, any more than saying that an event has physical causes is incompatible with saying it is caused by God. It is unbib- lical and philosophically groundless to insist it must be one or the other—either physical or spiritual—but not both.

In the next chapter, we will continue to look at arguments against the soul to see whether they are any more successful than PSA was at refuting the claim that we are a body-soul union.

7

Mind-Body Interaction
and Simplicity

In the "progress of science" argument, the frequent tactic is basically a matter of shaming dualists out of their dualism. When the progress argument is used in casual conversation, or even among people with significant experience and expertise in science, it may be treated as if it speaks for itself: the progress of science has gradually eliminated whatever is explanatorily extraneous, paring our view of nature—and ourselves—down to the bare physical foundations. In what follows we will consider a few refinements of those arguments, attempts to pinpoint what is supposed to make it almost impossible to believe in souls anymore.

The Interaction Argument
The first of these refinements is the interaction argument. In its most basic form, the argument says something like this: "If we suppose that the mind or soul is something immaterial, then it could not causally affect—or be causally affected by—the material brain. A soul cannot move a body, and a body cannot move a soul. They are different types of entities and could not possibly interact. How could they?"

This is sometimes expressed through a principle that "like only affects like." Matter can causally affect matter, but something immaterial could not. The problem with this objection to the causal interaction between matter and non-matter is that it is hard to see why anyone would *believe* the causal likeness principle, or how anyone who did believe it could hope to demonstrate its truth. It is certainly not a truth of logic or a truth of definition that matter can be affected only by matter. That is not what *matter* means— it does not mean "subject only to the influence of other matter." It is not a logical truth; nor is it something we have discovered by observation, so it is not a scientific truth either. No one has observed the causal likeness principle. It is purely a philosophical proposition, and it is hard to see what motivates it other than a basic, intuitive preference some people have for the material and a dislike for opening up the system of causal interaction to possible immaterial influences. It is pure prejudice.

On the other hand, while the causal likeness principle has precious little to recommend it despite its popularity, there is a somewhat more sophisticated way of stating an objection to interaction that does have at least a modicum of scientific support. The most interesting and challenging objection draws upon the principle of conservation of energy. The law of conservation of energy states that the total energy of an isolated system remains constant over time. One way this is often formulated is to say that energy cannot be created, nor can it be destroyed—it can only undergo changes in form. For example, the kinetic energy of a cannonball fired straight up in the air is converted to potential energy as the ball rises and slows; then as it begins to fall, the potential energy is converted back into kinetic energy. In addition, a small amount of heat energy is lost due to friction, but that energy does not disappear; it gets distributed among the air molecules that were exerting the friction force in the first place. Again, all of this is true only within an isolated system not receiving or losing energy to the outside.

In discussions of the soul or mind, conservation laws are used to argue that causal interaction between something physical and something immaterial is impossible. The reason is that causation is understood, on the physical level, as primarily involving changes in the momentum or position of some physical object, whether something small like a particle or something large like a bus. In the case of the interaction between mind and body, what we would need is for the immaterial mind to somehow bring about a change of state in the material brain, but such a change of state is possible only by imparting energy to the system to reposition the particles underlying the brain's structure. Without this kind of alteration, there would be no change in the state of the brain, and (the story goes) therefore no change in either the mental state of the agent or of the position or movements of the body.[1]

Let me illustrate with an example. Suppose while reading this you decide to set the book down and go make a cup of coffee, since everyone knows that's the best way to read a book. Because you decided to, an unfathomably complex cascade of events now begins: your brain initiates a series of chemical signals that lead to impulses throughout your body to contract some muscles and relax others, and constant feedback as to your location, orientation, balance, and environment is being processed at fantastic speeds. Even the most sophisticated machinery humanity has invented looks laughably clumsy when compared with the effortless elegance of human motion.

But the question arises, what initiated this mind-bogglingly complex sequence of events that led to the simple action of walking to the kitchen and brewing the coffee? On the one hand, the answer would have something to do with a state of the brain immediately preceding the decision—similar to the neural firing patterns we will discuss later that take place during free choices.

---

1. There are similar concerns about how body-to-mind causation would work, but the problems are different enough that we can ignore them for now and focus only on mind-to-body causation.

On the other hand, the truly obvious answer is that it was a *deci-sion made in your mind*. On the supposition that the mind or soul is involved in such operations, the conservation concern is how the mind could have the causal power to move the chemicals in the brain without violating a law. It seems that it would require energy to be imputed to the system of the brain; otherwise nothing could be moved, and nothing could start the physical process of setting the book down, rising from your chair, and going to the kitchen.

But do conservation laws really rule out any mind-body interaction? If we look a little more closely at the issues, the case seems inconclusive at best. The first consideration is that conservation of energy laws apply only to closed systems. A closed system is defined as one that has no input of energy from the outside, so by that definition a system in which a soul were able to contribute energy into a system would not actually be a *closed* system at all, and would not therefore be subject to conservation restrictions. That is, if souls affect bodies by some kind of energy transfer, the system of the brain is not closed, and no conservation laws are violated.

We may not want to think of souls as transferring energy into brains, though, and we probably do not need to. If a mind does not affect a body by transfer of energy, is there any other plausible account of causation that might leave the door open for mind-body interaction? The answer is absolutely yes. In fact, many such models of causation appear in both the philosophical and scientific literature.

Causation

When studying the philosophy of science, one does not need to read very much before discovering that there is no consensus on what we mean when we say *A causes B*—and that is putting it mildly! Numerous models of causation are on offer, each one with many plausible aspects, and each one with problems. It may be surprising that such an apparently simple notion, that of causation, should turn out to be so difficult, but there are few, if any, more intractable and perpetually controversial problems in all of philosophy. Even a cursory overview would require combing through centuries of work, and at the end one would be no closer to a clear answer. One would encounter the Humean view, developed by eighteenth-century Scottish philosopher David Hume. According to him, *A causes B* just means that we have always seen A followed by B, and our minds have a "propensity" to produce in us a feeling of expectation that the next time we see an A, it will also be followed by a B. Causation, then, would be nothing but observed regularities and psychologically irresistible but philosophically indefensible feelings.

We would also encounter the probabilistic view, which says that *A causes B* just means that B is more likely to occur given A than without A. It is not necessary on this telling to have B always follow A, which uncertainty is a desirable result in some ways. For example, smoking causes lung cancer—but not all smokers get lung cancer, and not all lung cancer is from smoking. There is another view, known as the "counterfactual" view, according to which *A causes B* just means that if A had not occurred, B would not have occurred either. There is also the "powers" view, where *A causes B* means that A exercises a power, and B is the resulting change of the state of an object.

In fact, the disagreement over the proper definition of causation is so extensive that there is not even consensus about what we call the "relata of causation"—what kinds of things are As and Bs? Are they events? Are they objects? Are they relations between universals? Even the briefest of overviews can help illustrate the relevant point here: there is no uncontroversial account in philosophy of science about the nature of causation. And most importantly, none of these models requires the transfer or conservation of energy.

The problem is not limited to philosophy either. Multiple models of causation are operating in scientific practice too, and they are also notoriously difficult to synthesize. For example, in psychology one might say that chronic stress is a cause of depression. In sociology one might say that religious practices cause community cohesion. A biologist could talk about heart disease being caused by poor diet and lack of exercise. At these higher levels we may talk about a lot of different causal factors without any of them requiring energy transfer. What, for example, is the energy transfer story that explains why a student's desire to excel in her studies causes her to stay up late reading? And would an explanation like that even be proper? If I buy flowers for my wife, the reductionist approach would insist that the purchase is fully explained only when we have exhaustively described all the chemical and physical events in the brain that preceded it. Yet it seems that such an explanation is not just incomplete but irrelevant. The real explanation is that I love my wife and want to bless her. If there is a further explanation of those facts, it seems it ought to be psychological or personal, not merely neurological. In other words, the chemical explanation is actually a pretty poor one. Philosopher Charles Taliaferro puts it well:

> Back to [the] claim about causal integration having to involve physical signals: we have the challenge . . . of identifying the boundaries of the physical, but if we stipulate that all and only material objects are spatial, and all and only nonspatial objects (things, events, states) are mental, why think that causation only occurs through spatial contact or between spatial objects? This simply seems question begging; there are multiple theories of causation that are not question begging such as counterfactual theories and nomological theories. Either could well accommodate the nonphysical/physical interaction as itself (at the most basic level), as direct, and as not requiring an intermediary causal mechanism.[2]

---

2. Charles Taliaferro, "The Promise and Sensibility of Integrative Dualism," in *Contemporary Dualism: A Defense*, ed. Andrea Lavazza and Howard Robinson (New York: Routledge, 2014), 201–2.

Continuing our thoughts about energy conservation and transmission, modern physics has revolutionized our thinking and corrected many plausible intuitions that turned out to be false. At the microscopic, atomic, and subatomic level, chemists and physicists deal with issues in causation where things get truly bizarre. We may think that this is the level where energy transfer would be most relevant, but even here—despite what we might have expected—we cannot insist on energy transfer being a part of causation. In fact, the most fundamental underlying theories in physics, relativity and quantum mechanics, do not abide by the conservation of energy restriction.

It is hard to argue with the success of the general theory of relativity and quantum mechanics. From cancer treatment to naval operations, from massive particle accelerators to the use of our cell phones, the physics that underlies much of our technology depends on these theories. They have been unquestionably successful, with predictions based on them verifying their claims again and again. So, what do these highly successful theories have to say about energy transfer during causation and the need for energy to always be conserved? In short, they simply do not require it.

In the case of general relativity, the issue has to do with gravity. We are all familiar with the effects of gravity, and we live with it all day, every day. We know that (at least in one sense) it is gravity that keeps us from floating around the room. In any meaningful sense of causation, it should be proper to say that gravity causes us to stay in contact with the ground. But according to general relativity, the gravitational energy in a region cannot be defined; and because it cannot be defined, it cannot be said to be conserved.

Furthermore, it would not be correct to describe gravitational energy as being transferred at all. As English physicist Sir Roger Penrose states it when dealing with a technical problem in gravity, "[There should be] an essential uncertainty, owing to the fact that even in classical general relativity there is difficulty with the energy concept for gravity. There is no local expression for gravitational energy."[3] Christian philosopher Robin Collins rightly points out one of the implications for our theory of dualism and the interaction objection:

> The non-conservation of energy in general relativity opens up another response a dualist could give to the energy-conservation objection. A dualist could argue that, like the gravitational field, the notion of energy simply cannot be defined for the mind, and hence one cannot even apply the principle of energy conservation to the mind/body interaction. The mind, like the gravitational field, could cause a real change in the energy of the brain without energy being conserved.[4]

In addition to the problems for dogmatism about energy conservation raised by general relativity, quantum mechanics has a monkey wrench of its own to throw into the works. In the words of philosopher of physics Roberto Torretti, quantum mechanics "famously made a mockery of causation" in the classical sense.[5] A well-established and oft experimentally verified theory known as Bell's theorem shows that there are correlations between quantum states that cannot be attributed to local interaction, and certainly not to an exchange of energy; to do so would require the energy to be transferred at superluminal (faster-than-light) speeds, which is impossible. The correlations cannot be due to energy exchange, so they would appear to be yet another exception to the conservation and energy transfer rules of classical physics. And furthermore, these quantum correlations are integral to our understanding of nature in the microscopic world. Quantum mechanics is foundational to physics, physics to chemistry, and chemistry to biol-

3. Roger Penrose, "Gravity's Role in Quantum State Reduction," in *Physics Meets Philosophy at the Planck Scale: Contemporary Theories in Quantum Gravity*, ed. Craig Callender and Mick Huggett (Cambridge: Cambridge University Press, 2009), 302.

4. Robin Collins, "The Energy of the Soul," in *The Soul Hypothesis: Investigations into the Existence of the Soul*, ed. Mark C. Baker and Stewart Goetz (New York: Bloomsbury Academic, 2011), 130.

5. Roberto Torretti, *Philosophy of Physics* (Cambridge: Cambridge University Press, 1999), 355.

ogy. What is true and well established at the quantum level is not merely an unimportant footnote to science at other levels; it is indispensable to it.

What both of these developments in twentieth-century physics show (first general relativity and then quantum mechanics) is that the plausible and commonly touted conservation of energy principles cannot be used to rule out real causal interactions that do not involve an exchange of energy in the usual sense. More specifically, they cannot pronounce causal relations between the soul and the body to be impossible either, even if no energy transfer is involved. If the causal connections cannot be detected or measured, there are still no grounds to say that science prohibits them. Modern physics has indeed "made a mockery of causation" and cannot be used as grounds for rejecting mind-body interaction. In the words of physicist and Anglican priest John Polkinghorne:

> It is a perfectly coherent and acceptable strategy to interpret physical unpredictabilities as signals of the presence of a causal openness, permitting the operation of causal influences over and above those resulting from the exchange of energy between constituents that has been the traditional story told by science. An obvious candidate for such an additional causal principle would be the willed acts of intentional human agents. Another possibility would be divine providential action, continuously operating within the open grain of nature. An honest science is not in the position to forbid either of these possibilities.[6]

The Slight-Changes Argument

Next we turn to what many think is the most potent argument for the materialism of persons. In fact, this argument alone accounts for most modern scientific objections to dualism. The argument is usually deployed casually, with a wave of the hand and a

---

6. John Polkinghorne, "The Universe as Creation," in *Intelligent Design: William A. Dembski and Michael Ruse in Dialogue*, ed. Robert B. Stewart (Minneapolis: Fortress, 2007), 169.

dismissive comment. So confident are its advocates that they can say things like this, from philosopher Michael Tooley:

> The fact that the belief that humans have immaterial minds is so often part of religious views of the world leads many people to think that that belief is not one that is open to scientific investigation. But that is a mistake. One can treat the proposition that humans have immaterial, rational minds as a scientific hypothesis, and then subject that hypothesis to scientific investigation. What happens when one investigates scientifically whether that hypothesis is true? The answer is that it turns out that there are excellent reasons for concluding that humans do not have immaterial minds.[7]

What compelling and powerful evidence has science discovered that could serve as such nearly conclusive proof against souls? The answer, in a word, is correlations. Minor changes in the brain can be correlated with changes in our mental life. The slight-changes argument, as we can name it, says that those connections between mind and brain are evidence that the brain is all there is—that our mental life is only a function of our brain states. If a soul is present and is supposed to be the seat of thought or the unifying first-person consciousness through which we experience our lives, then what would account for the detailed connections between brain states and mental states? Why would anything other than the brain and central nervous system be necessary? And if souls or immaterial minds are not necessary to understand our mental life, if they add nothing to the explanation, then we should eliminate them from our worldview.

It is well established that different regions of the brain correspond to different cognitive and motor abilities. If a patient has a tumor in the brain, neurologists can accurately predict the symptoms, based on the tumor's location. Maybe it will affect speech;

7. Michael Tooley, "Plantinga's New Argument against Materialism," *Philosophia Christi* 14, no. 1 (2012): 44.

maybe it will affect memory; maybe it will affect emotion regulation or control over the left side of the body. We can all attest to the impact that minute chemical changes can have on our perspective. Hunger, fatigue, fluctuations in hormones—all of these are well known to influence us. Whether from a cup of coffee, an allergy pill, or an antidepressant, we have all experienced these relationships between the chemical state of our bodies and the state of our minds. The correlations are so well understood that if certain symptoms manifest, the medical team may conclude that there is a problem in a certain region of the brain. They will know where to look. Materialists claim that these close connections would be surprising if the mind is immaterial but not surprising if a person is just a body (though, admittedly, a very complicated one). They say we would not find the life of the mind so dependent on the state of the brain.

Consider a few more examples. Suppose someone sustains a hard knock to the head and becomes unconscious. Why, if the mind is more than merely the brain, would that affect the person's ability to continue having thoughts and feelings? It might be understandable that the unconscious individual would be unable to control or influence his or her body—maybe the connections would become temporarily disabled until the body recovered. But why would *all thought life* cease during that period if the mind is not the brain? As we just noted, tumors, injuries, and brain damage due to disease affect mental life in predictable ways, depending on where they are located. Drugs and medications have an impact on our thought life, and they seem to do so by altering our brain chemistry. In addition, a person's mental life changes with age—but we might also wonder why aging and immaturity would have anything to do with our cognitive abilities. If the mind is a separate immaterial entity, why would it matter whether someone's brain were still maturing, fully developed, or deteriorating? We note a strong influence of inheritance too. Twins tend to have very similar tastes, moral judgments, and behaviors, even if they grow up separated from each other. Children tend to be similar in many ways to their parents. But why would genetics affect the immaterial soul?

Summarizing his reflections on these phenomena, Michael Tooley says:

> In short, there is a wealth of familiar phenomena that would be surprising and unexpected, and not at all what one would predict, and that would also be very hard indeed to explain, if the mind were an immaterial substance, but that all fall perfectly into place if the mind is, instead, the brain. There is, accordingly, very strong scientific evidence against the view that the mind is an immaterial substance.[8]

Is It Surprising?

Many people take this to be the strongest argument against dualism. If the mind is immaterial, it is (to them, anyway) surprising that there would be as much dependence on the state of the brain for the state of the mind as there undeniably is. On the other hand, if the mind is just the brain, they say that such dependence is exactly what we would anticipate. That is:

> We would not expect to find this sort of systematic, fine-grained dependence of consciousness and experience on patterns of neural activity if dualism were true. Why wouldn't we expect the kinds of dependencies revealed by neuroscience? If the dualist were correct, then not only would all conscious experience take place within a nonphysical subject, but additionally the kind of neural activity mapped out by the neurosciences should be explanatorily irrelevant to its occurrence and character. . . . So in the absence of strong reasons to expect otherwise, the fine-grained, neurobiological dependence of

---

8. Tooley, "Plantinga's New Argument against Materialism," 46.

consciousness make[s] physicalism a better fit with what we know from the neurosciences.[9]

The "surprise argument," as we can call it, says it would be improbable for the mind to depend so much on the brain if dualism were true. Since there is so much correlation between the mental and the physical, however, it is unlikely that anything more than the brain is involved in our mental life. The question, then, is this: how strong is the surprise argument?

The first thing to note is the probabilistic flavor of the argument. To say that some phenomenon is not what we would expect is to say something about how probable it would be, given other things we believe to be true. When we discuss probability, one option is to focus first on what is called *objective* probability. This is the kind of probability associated with rolling dice and tossing coins. The odds of rolling a one on a six-sided die is one in six; the probability of tossing two heads in a row in a coin toss is one in four, and so on. When we think of probability, especially when there is a number attached, we are usually thinking of it in light of statistics, frequencies, and other objective aspects. This is what people study when they take a probability and statistics class; it is the mathematical approach to determining the likelihood of something happening. Does the surprise argument express this kind of probability?

Plainly, no. When an advocate of the surprise argument says it would be unlikely that the mind would depend on the brain if dualism were true, he or she cannot be describing probability in its objective statistical sense. In order to utilize probabilities that way, we would need a lot of background experience with rational creatures having minds that just are brains, rational creatures having immaterial minds independent of brains, and rational creatures

---

9. Kevin Corcoran and Kevin Sharpe, "Neuroscience and the Human Person," in *Neuroscience and the Soul: The Human Person in Philosophy, Science, and Theology*, ed. Thomas M. Crisp, Steven L. Porter, and Gregg A. Ten Elshof (Grand Rapids, MI: Eerdmans, 2016), 129–30.

with minds dependent on brains. Then we would need to analyze our sample to see what percentage of those rational creatures had minds that were dependent on brains but also immaterial. Only if we found that proportion to be very small could we be justified in saying it is improbable. That is, first we would take the total number of rational creatures with immaterial minds that depend on brains and divide it into the total number of rational creatures—the sum of rational creatures with brains only, the rational creatures with independent immaterial minds, and the rational creatures with dependent immaterial minds. If we found that the number was very small, say less than 10 percent, then we could be justified in saying it is improbable to have a dependent immaterial mind. But again, that is plainly *not* what is being said. How would we gather those samples, even assuming that rational creatures of all three varieties exist? When the surprise argument avers that it would be unlikely for the mind to depend intimately on the brain, it cannot be based on objective probabilities.

But in addition to objective probabilities, there are *subjective* probabilities. The difficulty with them, though, is that they are, well, subjective. We often assign numbers even to subjective probabilities, but they are essentially reports of our confidence or credulity toward something. For example, someone might say he is 90 percent sure that a person he saw at the mall from a distance was a friend from high school. What is he saying, exactly? Is he saying that out of every hundred times he has seen someone who looked just like that, from that distance, he was right about it being an old friend ninety times? No. Rather, he is saying something like this: on a scale of one to a hundred, with a hundred being as certain as he can be and one being completely uncertain, he would score his confidence at ninety.

An alternative proposal is to think about it in terms of wagering: the probability or percentage corresponds to what I would be willing to wager that I am right. The higher the number, the more I would be willing to bet. When we say something is 50 percent probable in this sense, we mean we would lay even odds that it is true. When we say it is 100 percent certain, we mean we would wager any amount named. When we say there is a 0 percent chance, we are saying we would not take the bet even under the most favorable gambling conditions.

The notion of subjective probability, then, is simply to record our level of confidence that something is so. We sometimes assign numbers to those probabilities, but not because they are objectively or statistically valid; only because we need a scale to represent our confidence. This, it seems, is the kind of probability used in the surprise argument. When people say it is unlikely or improbable that the mind would depend closely on the brain if the mind were immaterial, they are reporting only that they would find that surprising and would be willing to wager against it being true.

The question, then, is the value of these self-reports of confidence levels. Granting that they are of some psychological or sociological interest, are they of any philosophical, scientific, or theological value in discerning the truth about human constitution? Alas, I suggest that they are not, for the following reasons.

First, what one person finds surprising is not binding on or transferable to anyone else. This is the very nature of subjectivity: one person has a reaction that another person may not. There is no right to impose on someone else one's own experience of surprise. Some people are, by nature, more easily surprised by things than others. Some are more skeptical; others are credulous or even gullible. What we find surprising will be highly contingent on our life experiences, family of origin, culture, and myriad other untraceable quirks. No two people will have exactly the same level of surprise about everything. In that way, reports of surprise are something like reports of having enjoyed or disliked a concert or a meal. As merely subjective descriptions, reactions of surprise are idiosyncratic. They are personally interesting data, but they have no power to demand the same reaction from someone else.

Second, science is full of things that are surprising even after they are well established. Quantum mechanics is an example of an extremely successful scientific theory, but one that is full of confusing and even troubling implications. There can be no doubt about how well it works, though; so, despite its strangeness, it is almost universally accepted as the best way to model what happens at the smallest scales. Even so, it is often seen as counterintuitive and surprising by those who study it. As Niels Bohr famously quipped, "Those who are not shocked when they first come across quantum theory cannot possibly have understood it."[10] Should it be discarded, then, since its conclusions are—using Tooley's words above—"surprising and unexpected, and not at all what one would predict, and . . . very hard indeed to explain"?

We need not use such exotic examples, either. It is very surprising to me that the table I sit at is almost totally empty space, made only of incredibly tiny charged particles separated by vast distances relative to their size. It is surprising to me that I can get one magnetic train car on a children's train track to move without touching it, pushing it, or pulling it merely by bringing another magnet close. It shocks me sometimes that things fall to the earth, or that we stay in orbit around the sun and that earth holds onto the moon, seemingly pulled by invisible strings. These examples move me to worship the Lord God, the Creator, whose power and wisdom are beyond imagining and who made all these things, holding them together at every moment by and through and for and in Jesus Christ—but it is hard to see how the reaction of surprise by these wonders has any bearing on their truth.

Third, it is difficult to see why it would not be at least as surprising that brains would lead to mental states as that there would be an immaterial mind related to the brain and body. When we think about the nature of a brain, that it is a collection of nothing other than matter collected from food and rearranged thereafter,

---

10. Niels Bohr, conversation with Werner Heisenberg, Copenhagen, June 1952, quoted by Heisenberg, *Physics and Beyond* (New York: Harper & Row, 1971), 206.

there would be nothing to suggest that such an arrangement could lead to conscious experience and a mental life. This, as we discussed earlier, is the hard problem of consciousness and one that is overlooked in the surprise argument. Even if we find it surprising that a mind and a body would exhibit so much interdependence, we could easily find it equally surprising that arranging bits of matter just so would cause consciousness and self-awareness to emerge as if life and thought were infused by magic into a golem made of clay.

Fourth, it should really be no more surprising now than it would have been in the past. We have continued to improve the details of the model, but the brain-mind connection has been known for centuries. Psychologist Daniel Robinson summarizes some of that history:

> Long before the period of modern medical science there was widespread recognition of mental or psychological disturbances arising from injuries to the head. The Smith papyrus, discovered in 1862 and dating to the sixteenth century BC, presents some 48 cases of which more than 30 describe neurological deficits traced to injuries of the skull, the brain and the spinal cord. For example, the papyrus associates both aphasia and loss of hearing with skull fractures in the area of the temporal cortex. The point is that recognition of the special relationship between the brain and various sensory, motor, and cognitive powers occurs quite early in the history of disciplined observations. What might be called *experimental* neurosurgery did not begin until the second century AD when Galen sectioned the recurrent laryngeal nerve of pigs to test the hypothesis that vocalization is localized in the throat. Pathologists, too, entered early in the development of the brain sciences. The Hippocratic texts of ancient Greece note that traumatic injuries to one side of the brain have behavioral effects on the contralateral side. A century later, the great anatomist, Herophilus, identified the brain as the organ of cognition

and perception and even distinguished between sensory and motor nerves.[11]

If people knew there was a relationship between the brain and our mental life before, but were still able to affirm the separability and substantiality of the mind anyway, why should it be any more strange or difficult for us today?

Along those lines, consider the following passages from René Descartes, published nearing four hundred years ago. Descartes is one of the thinkers most associated with mind-body dualism. In reflecting on the plausibility of believing in souls, given growing understanding of the brain, Descartes insisted that maintaining a dualist framework, while affirming the influence of the brain on the mind, was still both possible and appropriate. In his famous work *Meditations* or in his comments about them, he advocates for the union of soul and body and insists that the two are closely connected, even though they are separated substances whose union will one day be dissolved. The soul is not merely floating around in isolation from the body, but Descartes refers instead to the person as "the composite, that is, the mind united with this body."[12] As he states it, "I am not merely present in my body as a sailor is present in a ship, but I am very closely joined and, as it were, intermingled with it, so that I and the body form a single unit."[13] He says:

> For the fact that one thing can be separated from another by the power of God is the very least that can be asserted in order to establish that there is a real distinction between the two. Also, I thought I was very careful to guard against anyone inferring from this that man was simply "a soul which makes use of a body." For in the Sixth Meditation, where I dealt with

---

11. Daniel N. Robinson, "Minds, Brains, and Brains in Vats," in Baker and Goetz, *The Soul Hypothesis*, 52.

12. René Descartes, *The Philosophical Writings of Descartes*, trans. John Cottingham, Robert Stoothoff, and Dugald Murdoch, vol. 2 (Cambridge: Cambridge University Press, 1999), 59.

13. Descartes, *Philosophical Writings*, 2:56.

the distinction between the mind and the body, I also proved at the same time that the mind is substantially united with the body. . . .

Finally, the fact that "the power of thought is dormant in infants and extinguished in madmen" (I should not say "extinguished" but "disturbed"), does not show that we should regard it as so attached to bodily organs that it cannot exist without them. The fact that thought is often impeded by bodily organs, as we know from our own frequent experience, does not at all entail that it is produced by those organs. This latter view is one for which not even the slightest proof can be adduced.[14]

With amazing foresight, Descartes even addresses the objections we saw earlier from Tooley, about how a person's age and physical development are relevant to mental activity despite the mind's immaterial nature.

We are not, Descartes argues, souls that simply make use of our bodies; we are substantially united to them. So, nearly four centuries ago, he was able to say that "the whole mind seems to be united to the whole body" but is only *immediately* affected by the brain.[15] He recognized and even insisted that our mental life was going to be, in part, functionally intertwined with our brain so that the state of our brain was a significant factor in the state of our mind. He did not need MRIs or thermal imaging to know that; it was as apparent to him then as it is to us now.

In short, Descartes—just one example among many—demonstrates that there is *nothing* new in the so-called scientific objection to dualism that should threaten our belief that we are soulish creatures. Philosopher Stephen Evans summarizes it very well:

We did not need neurophysiology to come to know that a person whose head is bashed in with a club quickly loses his

---

14. Descartes, *Philosophical Writings*, 2:160.
15. Descartes, *Philosophical Writings*, 2:59.

or her ability to think or have any conscious processes. Why should we not think of neurophysiological findings as giving us detailed, precise knowledge of something that human beings have always known, or at least could have known, which is that the mind (at least in this mortal life) requires and depends on a functioning brain? We now know a lot more than we used to know about precisely *how* the mind depends on the body. However, *that* the mind depends on the body, at least prior to death, is surely not something discovered in the twentieth century.[16]

We continue to improve our understanding of the details, but the close connection between mind and body has been obvious for ages. The problem was not that people were ignorant of this connection in the past; the problem was—and is—that we do not sufficiently reflect on it for the simple reason that we do not notice it. We are so used to it that it gets taken for granted. Again, Descartes understood this: "I must admit, however, that the fact that the mind is closely conjoined with the body, which we experience constantly through our senses, does result in our not being aware of the real distinction between mind and body unless we attentively meditate on the subject."[17] The "very strong scientific evidence against the view that the mind is an immaterial substance" Tooley pointed to turns out to be nothing at all.

---

16. C. Stephen Evans, "Separable Souls: Dualism, Selfhood, and the Possibility of Life after Death," *Christian Scholar's Review* 34, no. 3 (2005): 333–34.
17. Descartes, *Philosophical Writings*, 2:160.

8

The Question of Freedom

When I was in seminary, I wrote a paper on the metaphysics of freedom for a philosophy of religion course. I started by laying out the two most prominent views of freedom, known as libertarianism and compatibilism. I asserted that most unbelievers would be drawn to libertarianism, as would many believers, but only a Christian—specifically one committed to a Reformed perspective on God's sovereignty and human freedom—would have reason to embrace compatibilism. In his comments on my paper, my professor disagreed, and since then I have seen his observation hold true time and again: I had the story backward. In fact, the overwhelming majority of secular philosophers hold to a form of compatibilism, and while it's true that many Christians also do for theological and biblical reasons (not just philosophical), it is much easier for a Christian than for a naturalist to be a philosopher and a libertarian about freedom. So, what are these two views of freedom, and why was my professor right?

Libertarianism

Let us take the two views in turn, starting with libertarianism. First, it is important to note that when we use the expression "libertarian" in discussions about the metaphysics of freedom, we mean nothing at all of what the word means in politics. In social and political philosophy, libertarianism is the view that there should be very little if any control over what people do, including and especially over actions that are potentially harmful to the person doing them but not directly dangerous to anyone else. For example, political libertarians might favor the deregulation of what they see as harmless or recreational tobacco, drug, or alcohol use; they might favor legalized prostitution; they might assert their right to ride a motorcycle without a helmet or drive a car without a seat belt. We need not concern ourselves at all with those questions here, though there are certainly many interesting discussions to be had on those topics.

The discussion here is focused on what it means to say that an action is done freely, and this is the kind of libertarianism I intend to consider. There are many ways of defining libertarianism, and some get quite technical. Indeed, making fine distinctions between different varieties of libertarianism has kept philosophers busy for generations and will undoubtedly continue to do so in the future. Still, a common core among them can be expressed as a kind of counterfactual power to do otherwise. A libertarian will say that *an action is done freely if it is possible for the agent (the person performing the action) to either do it or not do it.* The agent has the power to stop or go.[1] Without such a power, it is said, there is no freedom. Libertarian freedom requires the ability to do otherwise.

There can be very little doubt that, at least on some level, this definition seems to capture what we usually mean by freedom. As we shall see, however, it turns out that making it work will be a lot harder than it looks. As Samuel Johnson, eighteenth-century man of letters, once said, "All theory is against the freedom of the will;

---

1. This way of putting it comes from Daniel C. Dennett, e.g., in *Elbow Room: The Varieties of Free Will Worth Wanting* (Cambridge, MA: MIT Press, 1984), and *Freedom Evolves* (London: Penguin, 2007).

all experience for it."[2] We think that we have libertarian freedom, though describing how it is possible turns out to be difficult—and well-nigh impossible for materialists regarding human persons.

Compatibilism

The other main view of freedom is known as compatibilism. That might seem like a strange name, but the origin is in its affirmation of two apparently contradictory ideas: that we are free, and that we are determined to do the things we do. In other words, being free is compatible with being determined. Here there is no counterfactual power of *stop or go*; no requirement that the agent performing the action could have done otherwise. Instead, what makes an action free is simply that the agent performs it by choice. The thing done is what the agent wants and intends to do, even if wanting or intending something different is not possible for him or her. Maybe the agent could have chosen and thereby done otherwise after all. But it is not necessary that he or she could have chosen to.

There are two primary motivations for compatibilism. As a theological position, compatibilism is driven by the belief that God's sovereignty is meticulous, that he is in control—causal control, not just passively allowing or permitting—of everything that happens, including every human choice. There are ample biblical reasons for holding this position, and I will consider some of them later in this chapter. Anyone in the tradition of Augustine, Calvin, and Luther will generally hold this view, popularly known as the "Calvinist" position in the familiar Calvinism-Arminianism debate (though it might be better described as the Augustine-Pelagius debate, owing to their discussion of the same subject many centuries earlier).

The other motivation most decidedly does *not* arise from careful thinking about biblical texts and philosophical puzzles like

---

2. Quoted in James Boswell, *The Life of Samuel Johnson, LL.D.* (London: Charles Tilt, 1840), 417.

trying to reconcile God's foreknowledge of our actions with our performing them freely. Instead, it is that the causal closure of the universe under the laws of nature combined with the belief that human beings are merely material together entail that our actions must always be the unavoidable, ineluctable result of physical forces operating on prior arrangements of matter. If we are only matter, the state of our minds at any point is the direct result of the state of our brains at that point, but the state of our brains at any point is—like the state of any physical object—just whatever is entailed by its immediately previous state and the laws of nature. It is for this reason that Sam Harris describes us as "biomechanical puppets,"[3] a logical implication of something known as the "consequence argument."

The consequence argument points out the difficulty inherent in reconciling any form of libertarianism with physicalism. Remember that, according to a materialist view of personhood, the state of the brain is sufficient to determine the state of the mind: having a thought, desire, fear, intention, or any other mental event *just is* being in a certain brain state. At any moment the state of the brain, as a material object, is wholly determined or caused by the immediately preceding state of the brain, and what the laws of nature entail will result from that initial condition. Since we are not in control of the past, and we are not in control of the laws of nature, at no moment can we be in control of any of our thoughts, including the decisions we make, because they are just the consequences of other things we have no control over. It might *feel* like we deliberate over our choices and *feel* like we can choose between forks in our paths, but such things are merely illusions. Whether we stop or go is determined by what chemistry and physics say will happen next in the (admittedly very complicated) system of our brain. Our choices are just the consequences of things over which we have no control.

---

3. Sam Harris, *Free Will* (n.p.: Free Press, 2012), 47.

On the assumption that the mind is the brain, decision-making becomes just another physical event. Cornell philosophy professor Derk Pereboom describes it this way:

> If everything is wholly constituted of microphysical entities governed by deterministic laws, then the complete state of the physical universe at any time, together with these deterministic laws, renders inevitable every subsequent complete microphysical state of the universe. Again, if every subsequent complete microphysical state of the universe is rendered inevitable in this way, and everything is wholly microphysically constituted, then clearly every subsequent state of the universe is rendered inevitable in this way.[4]

And according to the materialist view of persons, everything *is* constituted of microphysical states or collections of microphysical states. This leads to not just one but two conceptually distinct kinds of determinism. In the words of J. P. Moreland, distinguished professor of philosophy at Talbot School of Theology,

> [Materialism] is deterministic in two senses: diachronically, such that the state of the universe at any time (t) coupled with the laws of nature determine or fix the chances for the state of the universe at subsequent times; synchronically, such that the features of and changes regarding macro-wholes are dependent on and determined by micro-physical phenomena.[5]

The determinism goes up—the structure and nature of the macroscopic object, such as a brain, is entirely a matter of the vast number of microstructures that make it up. And the determinism goes forward—what happens at time (t) determines what happens at every later time ($t+1$).

---

4. Derk Pereboom, *Living without Free Will* (Cambridge: Cambridge University Press, 2001), 73.

5. J. P. Moreland, "Theism, Robust Naturalism, and Robust Libertarian Free Will," in *The Naturalness of Belief: New Essays on Theism's Rationality*, ed. Paul Copan and Charles Taliaferro (Lanham, MD: Rowman & Littlefield, 2019), 231.

Yet there is noteworthy reason to back off a little on the determinism talk. According to the most successful theories of quantum physics, indeterminism is an inextricable feature of the world as well. Quantum indeterminacy is widely accepted, though not quite universally. Albert Einstein famously argued against it, but Alain Aspect's confirmation of Bell's inequalities in 1981 has convinced most physicists that indeterminism is not merely due to a lack of knowledge on our part—due, that is, to "hidden variables"—but also something that cannot be eliminated from quantum mechanics at all. Like most things in the physics of the very small, however, theories to the contrary abound. But it is pretty safe to say that there is a strong consensus in favor of some indeterminacy at the quantum level. Even so, this will not offer hope of rescuing libertarianism from the clutches of material determinism for at least two reasons. First, quantum effects get flushed out of large systems like brains. They are relevant only in very, very small systems. Second, such factors amount to little more than randomness, which no one thinks is sufficient for libertarian freedom anyway. So we are still safe in talking about determinism as the consequence of materialism, even while some quantum indeterminacy is acknowledged.

Making Decisions

At the level of functioning of a brain, scientists have carefully described what happens when we make decisions—at least, what happens in the brain that can be observed by the latest technologies. Their technical achievements are impressive, and the precision of modern instruments allows for incredibly detailed descriptions. Consider this one from Sam Harris:

> The physiologist Benjamin Libet famously used EEG to show that activity in the brain's motor cortex can be detected some 300 milliseconds before a person feels that he has decided to move. Another lab extended this work using functional

magnetic resonance imaging (fMRI): Subjects were asked to press one of two buttons while watching a "clock" composed of a random sequence of letters appearing on a screen. They reported which letter was visible at the moment they decided to press one button or the other. The experimenters found two brain regions that contained information about which button subjects would press a full 7 *to 10 seconds* before the decision was consciously made. More recently, direct recordings from the cortex showed that the activity of merely 256 neurons was sufficient to predict with 80 percent accuracy a person's decision to move 700 milliseconds before he became aware of it.[6]

Thus, Harris points out, it seems from these observations that the decisions we make come fairly late in the game. We might think we make a decision and then the brain responds to the decision we make. According to Harris, however, what happens is quite the reverse: the decision, as we are aware of making it, has really already been made and determined by the states of the brain immediately preceding it. What we call "making a decision" might feel like deliberation and an exercise of the will, but, says Harris, it really just amounts to our becoming aware of something that was already determined to happen and a process that is already well underway.

Other scientific accounts paint a similar picture. In *Psychology Today*, one author offered this description:

A February 2015 study, from the Okinawa Institute of Science and Technology (OIST) Graduate University in Japan, found that a key part of the brain involved in decision-making, called the striatum, appears to operate hierarchically within its three different sub-regions. The striatum is part of the basal ganglia, which makes up the inner core of the brain and processes both decision-making and subsequent actions. Neuroscientists divide the striatum into three regions: 1. Ventral (VS)

---

6. Harris, *Free Will*, 8–9.

2. Dorsomedial (DMS) and 3. Dorsolateral (DLS). Each region plays a distinctive role in: 1. Motivation 2. Adaptive Decisions and 3. Routine Actions, respectively. In an unexpected twist, the researchers at OIST found the three parts of the striatum work together in a coordinated hierarchy. Although the three different regions in the striatum have distinct roles, they ultimately harmonize and work together in different phases of decision-making.[7]

Thus, according to this view, decision-making—and therefore what we take to be the exercise of our will and the performance of free actions—is all just a result of complicated brain processes.

In more fMRI research, subjects were asked to play a game in which they tried to maximize their points by deciding how to combine three attributes—shape, color, and pattern—according to a set of rules. As they made their decisions, their brains were carefully monitored. Here is a summary of the researchers' findings:

We tested the hypothesis that interactions between regions of dorsolateral prefrontal cortex (dlPFC) and ventromedial prefrontal cortex (vmPFC) implicated in self-control choices would also underlie the more general function of context-dependent valuation. Consistent with this idea, we found that the degree to which stimulus attributes were reflected in vmPFC activity varied as a function of context. In addition, activity in dlPFC increased when context changes required a reweighting of stimulus attribute values. Moreover, the strength of the functional connectivity between dlPFC and vmPFC was associated with the degree of context-specific attribute valuation in vmPFC at the time of choice. Our findings suggest that functional interactions between dlPFC and vmPFC are a key aspect of context-dependent valuation and that the role of this network during choices that require self-control to adjudicate

7. Christopher Bergland, "The Neuroscience of Making a Decision," *Psychology Today*, May 6, 2015, https://www.psychologytoday.com/us/blog/the-athletes-way/201505/the-neuroscience-making-decision.

between competing outcome preferences is a specific application of this more general neural mechanism.[8]

While that is quite a mouthful, the trend emerges again clearly: making a decision is treated here as simply being in a brain state. Since being in a brain state is determined by previous states of intricate structures, external causal factors, and laws of nature, the result is determined by the inputs. Granted, the manner of determination is unimaginably complicated, and essentially unpredictable because of its complexity. Even so, the inputs determine the outputs. Listen again to Sam Harris:

> Decisions, intentions, efforts, goals, willpower, etc., are causal states of the brain, leading to specific behaviors, and behaviors lead to outcomes in the world. Human choice, therefore, is as important as fanciers of free will believe. But the next choice you make will come out of the darkness of prior causes that you, the conscious witness of your experience, did not bring into being.[9]

While some authors try to get around these implications by inventing new approaches such as property dualism, nonreductive physicalism, or some forms of emergentism, those efforts do not rest on any sort of evidential basis. They seem like little more than wishful thinking: a hope that somehow things are not really the way physicalism says they must be, and that a purely materialistic view of human nature can still be salvaged without having to sacrifice libertarian freedom. But atheist materialist philosopher Jaegwon Kim diagnoses the prospects of such a project well, calling belief in freedom and mental causation "an idle dream" if physicalism is true. "Reductive physicalism saves the mental but only as a part of the physical." As he recognizes, there can

---

8. Sarah Rudorf and Todd A. Hare, "Interactions between Dorsolateral and Ventromedial Prefrontal Cortex Underlie Context-Dependent Stimulus Valuation in Goal-Directed Choice," *Journal of Neuroscience* 34, no. 48 (2014): 15988–96.

9. Harris, *Free Will*, 34.

be no room for mental causation—"the causal powers of mental properties turn out to be just those of their physical realizers, and there are no new causal powers brought into the world by mental properties."[10] Your decision to raise your arm does not cause your arm to move—that would be a mental property with a causal power. While mental states feel like real powers, they are just emergent from the physical bases that actualize them. On a materialist account, a cold, hard truth would need to be confronted: either we are not free at all or we are free only in a compatibilistic sense.

Compatibilism and Christianity

Recall that compatibilism says that being free is compatible with being determined. According to that view, to be free means that an agent does an action because that action is chosen by the agent. The agent stops or goes, moves or stays because that is what he or she wants and chooses to do. On a materialist account, given the implication of determinism, we could still be free in this sense. Returning to the story about my professor, what he was referring to is the popularity of this position among materialist philosophers. They see the implication of determinism but also know from experience that we genuinely seem to deliberate and make choices. Compatibilism allows us to affirm the reality of both.

So one might wonder at this point, would that be so bad? What would it mean for Christianity if secular scientists and philosophers successfully and convincingly advocate for compatibilism as the only way to understand the latest developments in cognitive science? Would the Christian worldview be threatened?

The answer seems clear: not at all. In fact, much of the history of Christian thought on this subject has been along compatibilistic lines. As most Christians recognize, there is ample biblical support for what is known popularly as the Calvinist picture (and many

---

10. Jaegwon Kim, *Mind in a Physical World: An Essay on the Mind-Body Problem and Mental Causation* (Cambridge, MA: MIT Press, 2000), 118–20.

argue that there is also ample support for the Arminian position, but we will look at that separately). Jesus said, "No one can come to me unless the Father who sent me draws him" (John 6:44). We do not come to him in our own power or as a result of our own initiative—we come because we are drawn in. As Paul says in Ephesians 1:4–5, "[God] chose us in [Christ] before the foundation of the world, that we should be holy and blameless before him. In love he predestined us for adoption to himself as sons through Jesus Christ, according to the purpose of his will." Our coming to him was not ultimately *our* choice but *God's* choice—a choice made in eternity past. Likewise, Jesus says to his disciples, "You did not choose me, but I chose you . . . that you should go and bear fruit" (John 15:16). Jesus also says, "All that the Father gives me will come to me" (John 6:37), indicating that the movement from death to life in salvation is a sovereign work of God that cannot fail. As John describes it elsewhere, it is like being born, "not of blood nor of the will of the flesh nor of the will of man, but of God" (John 1:13). In Acts, Luke tells us that "when the Gentiles heard [the gospel], they began rejoicing and glorifying the word of the Lord, and as many as were *appointed* to eternal life believed" (Acts 13:48). Peter also expresses this perspective, saying that those who reject the gospel message "stumble because they disobey the word, as they were destined to do. But you [who believe] are a chosen race" (1 Pet. 2:8–9).

Perhaps the strongest statement of this perspective comes from Paul the apostle. Speaking of the Jews who resist the message of the Messiah, he raises the question of fairness—the biggest objection to compatibilism. That is, how can it be fair to hold people accountable for decisions that have causes in the will of God?

> What shall we say then? Is there injustice on God's part? By no means! For he says to Moses, "I will have mercy on whom I have mercy, and I will have compassion on whom I have compassion." So then it depends not on human will or exertion,

but on God, who has mercy. For the Scripture says to Pharaoh, "For this very purpose I have raised you up, that I might show my power in you, and that my name might be proclaimed in all the earth." So then he has mercy on whomever he wills, and he hardens whomever he wills. (Rom. 9:14–18)

In a surprising response to the objection he anticipates, Paul says:

You will say to me then, "Why does he still find fault? For who can resist his will?" But who are you, O man, to answer back to God? Will what is molded say to its molder, "Why have you made me like this?" Has the potter no right over the clay, to make out of the same lump one vessel for honorable use and another for dishonorable use? What if God, desiring to show his wrath and to make known his power, has endured with much patience vessels of wrath prepared for destruction, in order to make known the riches of his glory for vessels of mercy, which he has prepared beforehand for glory—even us whom he has called? (Rom. 9:19–24)

Later in the same discourse, he adds, "God has not rejected his people whom he foreknew. . . . The elect obtained [salvation], but the rest were hardened" (Rom. 11:2, 7). And he makes it clear that the calling is efficacious when he says, "For the gifts and the calling of God are irrevocable" (Rom. 11:29). The words of John, Luke, Peter, Paul, and Jesus himself quoted in these passages are the reason that many Christian theologians have embraced compatibilism. While we are free and do what we choose, even to the point of moral responsibility, our choices ultimately emerge from the inscrutable eternal decree of God the Father.

In addition to these biblical authors, some of the most important theologians in church history have promoted something like compatibilism—people as noteworthy as Saint Augustine of Hippo, John Calvin, and Martin Luther. Augustine (354–430) argued that humanity had begun free with the ability to choose either good or evil but, through sin, had lost the ability to choose good. As a result, "freedom" in a fallen state refers only to our being the author of our evil, rebellious actions—we do not have freedom in the sense of being able to choose good. Absent the regenerative grace of God, then, doing what God commands is not possible—yet Augustine claimed we freely choose the disobedience we cannot avoid. In a similar vein, Martin Luther (1483–1546), himself trained in the Augustinian tradition, and John Calvin (1509–1564) also argued that we are free but, at the same time, bound by sin.[11] Known for launching the Protestant Reformation, these two men shared a view of sin and utter dependence on God that was based on Scripture rather than tradition. One theologian puts it this way:

> The Reformers reacted negatively to the moralistic optimism of medieval theology and insisted on a pessimistic view of the human will in its state of sin. Martin Luther and John Calvin both wrote works on the *Bondage of the Will* that emphasized how sin has eradicated free will so that people will not choose God of their own free volition. If people are to be saved, God must enable them; yet he enables some and not others. Therefore, believing in God is the work of God who activates faith in the believer by his sovereign choice.[12]

More recently, the reflections of C. S. Lewis on his own conversion sound remarkably similar to this dual affirmation: we do things freely because we choose them, even though in many ways it would not make sense to say we could have chosen otherwise. Lewis would not have consented to being called a compatibilist, but the way he talks certainly seems to fit that description well. Listen to him recount the evening of his conversion:

---

11. It should be noted, however, that Luther and Calvin differed significantly in their views on this subject, especially when it comes to "irresistible grace." For a nice overview on this, see Douglas Sweeney, "Was Luther a Calvinist?," The Gospel Coalition, July 15, 2014, https://www.thegospelcoalition.org/article/was-luther-a-calvinist/.

12. Michael A. Bird, *Evangelical Theology: A Biblical and Systematic Introduction* (Grand Rapids, MI: Zondervan, 2013), 521–22.

In a sense I was not moved by anything. I chose to open, to unbuckle, to loosen the rein. I say "I chose," yet it did not really seem possible to do the opposite. On the other hand, I was aware of no motives. You could argue that I was not a free agent, but I am more inclined to think that this came nearer to being a perfectly free act than most that I have ever done. Necessity may not be the opposite of freedom, and perhaps a man is most free when, instead of producing motives, he could only say, "I am what I do."[13]

When we reflect on our own experiences, we see that what we choose is not merely random. It is the manifestation of our desires at that time, and the desires we have do not pop into existence from nowhere. They are the culmination of countless biological, environmental, genetic, personal, spiritual, psychological, neuro-chemical, and other factors. That is to say, when we act, we act for reasons. We do not need to insist that freedom requires the ability to do otherwise, because the ability to do otherwise would mean that at the time we make the decision—holding constant all those myriad factors just listed, and more—we could have made a different choice. But how? And why would we want that? To act in that way would seem simply random and purposeless, not free (and that is why my comment earlier about quantum indetermi-nacy does not offer help here). As one philosopher reasoned, if we insist that we could have done differently even in light of all those starting conditions being the way they were, "The conception that now emerges is not that of a free man, but of an erratic and jerking phantom, without any rhyme or reason at all."[14]

All of that goes to make a fairly simple but important point. The modern picture science delivers us, especially from the mate-rialist perspective held by most people working in neuroscience, psychology, and cognitive science, is one of a causally closed sys-

---

13. C. S. Lewis, *Surprised by Joy: The Shape of My Early Life* (New York: Harcourt, Brace & World, 1955), 224–25.
14. Richard Taylor, *Metaphysics* (Englewood Cliffs, NJ: Prentice-Hall, 1974), 51.

tem that therefore operates deterministically. One can certainly be a Christian and reject the picture of compatibilism I have just described, and in fact many Christians now and throughout church history *do* reject it. But insofar as the compatibilist perspective endorsed by materialists for *scientific* reasons is also consistent with a compatibilism endorsed by many Christians for *theological* reasons, there is nothing in this aspect of the materialist view of persons to threaten any orthodox Christian beliefs. Christianity can work very well even with the direst descriptions of determinism on offer.

Libertarianism, Christianity, and Souls

As I've noted, however, many Christians have espoused libertarian freedom, insisting that the only way we can be morally responsible for our actions is if we had the power of *stop and go*. Since God will judge us, it must be that we are morally responsible, or God himself would be unjust; so it must be that we have libertarian freedom. The advocates for this position have often lined up directly opposite the men we looked at earlier. For example, Pelagius opposed Augustine on this topic, and Jacobus Arminius (where we get "Arminianism") and his followers argued against the Lutheran/Calvinist position in their "Five Articles of Remonstrance." To them, generally speaking, God's foreknowledge and predestination are matters of God knowing in advance who would follow him and basing their election on that foreknowledge. In addition, they have insisted that we are really free to sin or not sin—a power that we must have to make sense of what God expects of us. Theologian Millard Erickson states: "Pelagius even held that it is possible to live without sinning. Would God have commanded, 'Be holy because I, the Lord your God, am holy' (Lev. 19:2), and 'Be perfect, therefore, as your heavenly Father is perfect' (Matt. 5:48), if sinlessness were not a possibility for human beings?"[15]

---

15. Millard J. Erickson, *Christian Theology*, 3rd ed. (Grand Rapids, MI: Baker, 2013), 844.

Choice is not predestined but made freely by us and owned wholly by us, because we truly have the power to perform or not perform our actions.

And it is not only Christian theologians who think we have libertarian freedom. While many materialist philosophers and scientists have recognized that physicalism leads to determinism, most people find that a very hard pill to swallow. It just feels like we are not determined and that we have the counterfactual power of choice. Simply put, the argument from experience trumps the argument from science and philosophy. In the tension pointed out above by Dr. Johnson, "All theory is against the freedom of the will; all experience for it." When it comes to choosing sides, most people will prefer experience over theory and affirm libertarianism.

This is where Christianity can have an advantage. If work in brain and cognitive science leads to determinism because it starts with materialism as an assumption, the way to get out of the net is to reject that materialist starting point. As we have considered, the soul as an immaterial substance with causal power can serve as the locus of libertarian control, since it lies outside the web of material causes. Its actions are not determined by the laws of nature. If there is any chance of rescuing libertarianism, it would be by getting the soul back into the picture, allowing real causal power for the mental and enabling that causal power to operate in an undetermined fashion. Materialism cannot support libertarian freedom, but dualism can.

Along these lines, J. P. Moreland summarizes the arguments of many leading philosophers:

> It is evident to most analytic philosophers who are philosophical naturalists that their ontological framework rules out, or at least, makes highly implausible, the reality of libertarian freewill and agency. As Kevin Timpe and Jonathan D. Jacobs correctly observe: "There is . . . a near consensus on this: naturalism is certainly incompatible with libertarian free

will." Thus, Roderick Chisholm claimed that "in one very
strict sense of the terms, there can be no science of man."
Along similar lines, John Searle says that "our conception of
physical reality simply does not allow for radical [libertarian]
freedom." And . . . John Bishop frankly admits that "the idea
of a responsible agent, with the 'originative' ability to initiate
events in the natural world, does not sit easily with the idea of
[an agent as] a natural organism.[16]

As we have seen, the traditional Christian doctrine of humanity teaches that we are body-soul unions, and that the existence
of an immaterial soul causally united with the body is the only
viable way to preserve libertarian freedom. As such, Christian
anthropology is vindicated over naturalism if we really do have
counterfactual freedom. In our earlier discussion about whether
freedom is possible given materialism, we noted the interpretation
of experiments favored by some scientists who think that the prior
activation of brain states before the subject is conscious of making
a decision shows that our intentions do not cause our actions. But
that is not the only possible interpretation of the data. Richard
Swinburne, an Oxford philosopher and Christian, notes that the
science is consistent with causation from a mind or soul affecting
the body. In fact, the assumption that our intentions do not lead
to our actions actually undermines the interpretation of those
who deny mental causation, since it depends on the test subjects'
reports on their experience as a result of their intention to do so.
As Swinburne points out:

> They are right to rely on this apparent testimony if they are
> right to believe that the subjects' past intentions to move their
> hand caused their later belief that they had that intention when
> the clock was recording [the number they report]. . . . So all
> [these] experiments designed to show that mental events do

not cause physical events require the experimenter to assume that sometimes mental events *do* cause physical events.[17]

Thus, they have to assume something is true in order to show that it is false, which entangles them in a contradiction.

Even more importantly, there is a compelling argument for the existence of God based on robust libertarian freedom. Given that libertarianism requires immaterial minds, we can ask whether naturalism or Christian theism offers a better metaphysical framework for the existence of those minds. In short, there is nothing in naturalism that can plausibly give rise to the mental—minds, spirits, or souls—but in Christian theism we already have an example in God of a libertarian-free spiritual Being who can causally interact with the material world. Moreland comments: "Therefore, it is hardly surprising that embodied or unembodied finite libertarian agents should exist in the world. But on a naturalist view, mental entities are so strange and out of place that their existence (or regular correlation with physical entities) defies adequate explanation."[18] If we have reason to believe we have libertarian freedom, then we have reason to believe we have souls. But if we have souls, we have reason to believe that the naturalistic worldview is wrong. Christian theism, on the other hand, easily accounts for them, and so it is explanatorily superior.

To summarize this tour through the metaphysics of freedom, we have seen a few vital points. First of all, if the consensus understanding of how to interpret cognitive science is right, then a compatibilist account of freedom is the only viable one. That view says freedom is compatible with determinism, because all it means to perform an action is to *own* it—to do or not do something because we desire and choose to. But compatibilism is perfectly acceptable to orthodox Christianity and has been the view of freedom favored by some of the tradition's most important thinkers.

---

17. Richard Swinburne, *Are We Bodies or Souls?* (Oxford: Oxford University Press, 2019), 135–36.
18. Moreland, "Theism, Robust Naturalism, and Robust Libertarian Free Will," 221.

The brain sciences pose no threat to their understanding of Christianity. On the other hand, if compatibilism is flawed and fails to capture what we really mean by freedom, then libertarianism is the right framework. It can function, however, only if we *reject* the materialist consensus and embrace some form of substance dualism to allow for real causal power and counterfactual freedom.

Souls can have no place in a naturalistic picture of the world, though, and there is no believable narrative of where they could emerge from or what could account for them. They would, however, fit very nicely with the existence of God and comport with what the Bible says about his role as Creator and our nature as creatures. The final score, then, either is tied—with Christianity suffering no damage at all from the attack of the naturalists— or shows the Christian point of view scoring a decisive victory over physicalism.

9

Reason, Science, and Morality

We have already reviewed the development of cognitive science of religion and some of the prominent naturalistic explanations for the phenomenon of religious belief. In that overview we spent a little time thinking through the consequences of the central claims of CSR, but in this chapter we will look more closely at problems that start to emerge with the naturalistic approach to religion advocated by many in the secular academy.

Trusting Science

First we will turn to the ways in which a naturalistic evolutionary approach to the cognitive science of religion undermines our confidence in the conclusions of science—including the very conclusions that cognitive scientists wish us to embrace. If naturalistic scientists are right, in other words, they will have undermined their own plausibility and our ability to *know* that they are right.

The history of science is long and interesting, not least of all because it is still not totally clear what counts as science and what does not. We have visited these issues in some of the foundational chapters early, but it is important to remember that science as a special, privileged way of knowing is a relative latecomer to the

intellectual landscape. Certainly it is only in its infancy as the supposed foundation to all knowledge and in its role as the ultimate
arbiter of all truth claims. Yet, from casual conversations in coffee
shops to serious scholarly presentations on public television or in
university lecture halls, it is abundantly common to hear that the
only way to really know something is to understand it scientifically. There is a lot of disagreement about what that even means;
about what it takes for something to count as science. There is
simply no consensus about what actually counts as science and
what crosses over into interpretation or even wild speculation.
I've discussed many of these issues in depth already, but it is worth
thinking about them again, if only briefly.

Some features that are commonly taken to be characteristics
of science are not thought to be present in nonscientific fields.
Chief among them is that science pertains to what is observable. If
something can be seen with the eyes, heard with the ears, touched
with the hands—these are the paradigm examples of observability.
Nowadays much of our observing in scientific settings is only indirectly done with the human senses, inasmuch as machines do most
of the detecting for us or at least act as intermediaries between us
and the objects we study; all the more so if the objects are very
small, moving very fast, or very far away. But the machines are
really just extensions of our senses.

Furthermore, it is presumed that scientific claims are publicly
accessible, are repeatable, and lead to predictions that can be
verified or falsified. In a highly publicized court case, *McLean
v. Arkansas Board of Education*, the topic was whether Intelligent Design could be treated as science and taught as part of the
public-school science curriculum. Not surprisingly, much of the
discussion centered on what counts as science, and to that end
the judge in the case, William Overton, established criteria to distinguish science from nonscience and pseudoscience. His criteria
for science were these: (1) it is guided by natural law, (2) it has
to be explanatory by reference to natural law, (3) it is testable

against the empirical world, (4) its conclusions are tentative (i.e., are not necessarily the final word), and (5) it is falsifiable.[1]

We could hardly overstate how much discussion these criteria invite. Every point is contentious, and every significant term is vigorously debated in the philosophical literature; nevertheless, many people consider these criteria broadly plausible and helpful as a starting point. All we need to notice here is that science, according to these restrictions, must be *naturalistic and empirical.*

A Christian might well argue that no scientific explanation could be complete on these grounds, because any explanation would be lacking if it omitted the role of God in creating and sustaining all that exists at every moment. It is as if we were describing the American approach to government but prohibited from referring to the Founding Fathers or the Constitution. Judge Overton's ruling would also require that even if God is involved in those ways, scientific consideration of his deeds must be confined to behind-the-scenes, invisible action and could never make reference to more direct or obvious ways God might have acted. At any rate, we can satisfy ourselves with saying that these restrictions are philosophically naive and theologically prejudiced. They do, however, bring a few key notions into the discussion—especially with the role they give to natural law in science: unless something is guided by natural law and explained in terms of natural laws, it could not count as science.

The problem with this is not immediately obvious, nor is its connection to the questions about God and brains with which we are now concerned. How does the natural law restriction factor into our discussion of human nature, minds, brains, and knowledge? The problem, in a word, is *induction.*

Inductive reasoning is usually contrasted with deductive reasoning (though the distinction does not always hold up). Paradigm cases of deduction would include things like concluding *Socrates*

---

1. *McLean v. Arkansas Board of Education,* 529 F. Supp. 1255 (E.D. Ark. 1982), sec. 4(c).

was mortal from the starting premises *Socrates was a man* and *All men are mortal.* With deduction, the failure or success of an argument is determined by whether the premises, if they are true, entail the conclusion. If we are told Joe has a sister, then we can deduce Joe has a sibling, because all sisters are siblings.[2] With deduction, a valid argument guarantees the truth of its conclusion—assuming, again, the truth of its premises. It would be impossible (in some sense) to have true premises, valid deduction, and a false conclusion.

With induction, the story is different. Inductive reasoning is based on probabilities, unlike deduction, so even a strong inductive argument makes its conclusion only *likely.* The stronger the argument, the more likely the conclusion is; strength often comes from a plurality of examples and observations. Myriad issues are raised by induction, and countless truly vexing puzzles. We will simply assume for our purposes here that inductive reasoning provides a generally reliable guide, and note that it is the method of reasoning used in science. When scientific conclusions are reached, it is through making observations, framing hypotheses that seem to explain those observations, and then testing the hypotheses by trying to verify or falsify the predictions it leads to. This procedure was what Judge Overton had in mind with the last three criteria, and his verdict that science holds conclusions tentatively is a recognition of the limits of induction.

We are often told that science is the paradigm method of knowing, and we have examined this claim already. But it is abundantly clear upon reflection that many conditions are needed for science to be possible in the first place. Philosophers Garrett DeWeese and J. P. Moreland list a few of those presuppositions of science:

---

2. No funny business is allowed! We cannot, for example, say, "By sister I mean a nun, and some of them have no siblings." The range of meaning for a word has to be restricted by context; that is the sort of thing I mean by saying logic is more nuanced than it seems. But we will simply skate by those problems here.

- the existence of a theory-independent, external world
- the orderly nature of the external world
- the knowability of the external world
- the existence of truth
- the laws of logic and mathematics
- the reliability of our cognitive and sensory faculties to serve as truth gatherers and as sources of justified beliefs in our intellectual environment
- the adequacy of language to describe the world
- the existence of values used in science (e.g., "test theories fairly and report test results honestly")
- the uniformity of nature and induction[3]

Taking only the last example, induction assumes the uniformity of nature. It assumes that things are going to behave the same when we observe them and when we don't; whether they are on earth or another planet; whether the experimenter is young or old, black or white, male or female. Now, it is worth saying that all of the assumptions listed above are *good* assumptions. They are justified and we are right to accept them. However, they are presuppositions of science and not things that scientific methods can actually establish. They are the foundations of science, not the conclusions of science. That is why John Kekes can say "philosophy, and not science, is a stronger candidate for being the very paradigm of rationality."[4]

Naturalism Falls Short

We now have a clearer picture of the cognitive foundations of science, so we are poised to ask an important question: Can a naturalistic approach to CSR provide those foundations?

Alas, it seems that it cannot. Given what we have seen about the foundations of science, we note at least two things: that these

---

3. Garrett J. DeWeese and J. P. Moreland, *Philosophy Made Slightly Less Difficult: A Beginner's Guide to Life's Big Questions* (Downers Grove, IL: InterVarsity Press, 2005), 136–37.
4. John Kekes, *The Nature of Philosophy* (Totowa, NJ: Rowman & Littlefield, 1980), 158, quoted by DeWeese and Moreland, *Philosophy Made Slightly Less Difficult*, 136.

foundations bear similarities to religious beliefs that should trouble the naturalist, and that whatever critics do to discredit religious beliefs also serves to discredit scientific beliefs.

The scientific belief–supporting structures I have described above all involve significant commitments to unverifiable claims based solely on "what seems to be the case." It *seems* like we can trust our senses; mathematics *seems* to work and make sense; it *seems* like nature is regular and that induction is reasonable and that we ought to report our findings honestly. But each of those claims is unverifiable directly. No experiment can show that experiments are a good way to discover things. Clearly most of us, even after reflecting on it, will decide to maintain these beliefs and affirm their reliability. Even so, despite our confidence, we have no objective, theory-independent way to confirm them.

In fact, these beliefs have the same traits as the "blind faith" Richard Dawkins attacks: they are beliefs in the absence of any evidence. Without referring to any sensations, how could we *demonstrate* that we can trust our senses? Apart from an appeal to what René Descartes called "the inner light of reason," how can we prove the axioms of mathematics? Simply put, we cannot. These things come on us with force and conviction, and they make sense of the world. They provide a cognitive framework for all kinds of useful investigations, and they ground the way we see and understand the world—even our human relationships. They, too, could be described as the mere by-products of evolutionary processes that care not a whit for truth, but have entirely different criteria for success.

Those who dismiss religious beliefs on the grounds that they cannot be demonstrated or proved to be true might have a point, but in making their point they fail to see that many of their most basic and important assumptions share all those same troubling features. Therefore, in attacking them, they attack the possibility of success in science; but the success of science is supposed to provide all the proof they need. A building is never more secure than its foundations, though, so dismissing religious claims because they are not scientific will ultimately require dismissing science because it is not scientific either. Religion is under attack because it appeals to unverifiable universals; transcendent, abstract laws of morality; a hermeneutical spiral that is dismissed as viciously circular—in general, believing in foundational principles that cannot be empirically verified. In each case, however, the scientific enterprise requires the same things.

What we see is that most of our beliefs, including beliefs about all sorts of scientific things and everyday beliefs, would also be "accidental" by-products of our cognitive systems in exactly the same way as beliefs about God are: natural selection would not favor individuals who were able to do quantum mechanics or calculus. We are able to form beliefs about quantum mechanics and calculus—as well as many other things—because our cognitive mechanisms, which would have originally evolved to do something else, are flexible enough to process different inputs.[5]

So we are reminded of Jesus's words to another group of antagonists: "'Let him who is without sin among you be the first to throw a stone.' . . . But when they heard it, they went away one by one" (John 8:7, 9).

But it is not only science that will be in danger. The significance of this argument extends even further, ensnaring all of reason in the net. No rational process or way of knowing will be safe if we are cut off in principle from knowing things that cannot be proved through sensory perception. Without some unverifiable assumptions and unobservable foundations, *all* knowledge will be impossible. As philosopher Alvin Plantinga argues, it is not *science and Christianity* that are incompatible and locked in a death struggle—it is *science and naturalism*:

The basic idea of my argument could be put (a bit crudely) as follows. First, the probability of our cognitive faculties being

5. David Leech and Aku Visala, "The Cognitive Science of Religion: A Modified Theist Response," *Religious Studies* 47, no. 3 (2011): 305.

reliable, given naturalism and evolution, is low. (To put it a bit inaccurately but suggestively, if naturalism and evolution were both true, our cognitive faculties would very likely not be reliable.) But then according to the second premise of my argument, if I believe both naturalism and evolution, I have a *defeater* for my intuitive assumption that my cognitive faculties are reliable. If I have a defeater for *that* belief, however, then I have a defeater for *any* belief I take to be produced by my cognitive faculties. That means that I have a defeater for my belief that naturalism and evolution are true. So my belief that naturalism and evolution are true gives me a defeater for that very belief; that belief shoots itself in the foot and is self-referentially incoherent; therefore I cannot rationally accept it. And if one can't accept both naturalism and evolution, that pillar of science, then there is serious conflict between naturalism and science.[6]

If naturalistic evolution is right, we have no reason to believe that *any* of our cognitive faculties or processes moves us closer to truth—and any argument that they would do so must depend on assuming that they are already reliable and that the arguments they lead us to endorse are trustworthy. It assumes that what we judge as solid reasoning really is solid, but it leaves us no resources for judging the weak from the strong. Even Charles Darwin noticed this with his "horrid doubt" when he said: "But then with me the horrid doubt always arises whether the convictions of man's mind, which has been developed from the mind of the lower animals, are of any value or at all trustworthy. Would any one trust in the convictions of a monkey's mind, if there are any convictions in such a mind?"[7]

C. S. Lewis made a similar observation on how a materialistic, naturalistic evolutionary account of human origins undermines reason:

---

6. Alvin Plantinga, *Where the Conflict Really Lies: Science, Religion, and Naturalism* (New York: Oxford University Press), 314.

7. Charles Darwin, letter to William Graham, July 3, 1881, in *The Complete Life and Letters of Charles Darwin*, ed. Taylor Anderson (n.p.: CreateSpace, 2018), 136.

Supposing there was no intelligence behind the universe, no creative mind. In that case, nobody designed my brain for the purpose of thinking. It is merely that when the atoms inside my skull happen, for physical or chemical reasons, to arrange themselves in a certain way, this gives me, as a by-product, the sensation I call thought. But, if so, how can I trust my own thinking to be true? It's like upsetting a milk jug and hoping that the way it splashes itself will give you a map of London. But if I can't trust my own thinking, of course I can't trust the arguments leading to Atheism, and therefore have no reason to be an Atheist, or anything else. Unless I believe in God, I cannot believe in thought: so I can never use thought to disbelieve in God.[8]

Unguided evolution would have no reason to favor true beliefs—only beliefs that promote the passing on of genetic material. If true beliefs work, then fine; but if false beliefs work just as well, then that is fine too. We simply have no principled reason to start our inquiries—into God, science, or anything else—by assuming that our doxastic instincts provide real evidence for the beliefs they generate. Maybe they do. But *if* they do, they require much better justification than evolutionary naturalism could ever provide.

Trouble for Morality

As troubling as the devastation to our ability to reason would be, it is not only reason that suffers under the worldview of the evolutionary naturalist. At least as troubling are the repercussions for morality. Just as our faculties may not have developed to aim at truth in reasoning, they also may be wildly inaccurate when leading us to believe in the truth of objective moral goodness.

First I should clarify that atheists can and often do act morally. There are many examples of unbelievers doing the right thing, even when it is difficult and even without any belief in God or the

---

8. C. S. Lewis, "They Asked for a Paper," in *Is Theology Poetry?* (London: Geoffrey Bles, 1962), 164–65.

moral structure he provides. They do it not to honor God or for an eternal reward but because they know it is right. The Scriptures themselves speak about this when Paul says:

> Indeed, when Gentiles, who do not have the law, do by nature things required by the law, they are a law for themselves, even though they do not have the law. They show that the requirements of the law are written on their hearts, their consciences also bearing witness, and their thoughts sometimes accusing them and at other times even defending them. (Rom. 2:14–15 NIV)

The apostle is pointing out that, in addition to *doing* what is right, they even *know* what is right. "The requirements of the law are written on their hearts." They have the innate awareness of morality that is essentially universal. Christian teaching is that this universal moral knowledge reflects the image of God and is there so that we might know him and live for him. It is biblical, therefore, to affirm that even unbelievers can (and usually do) have moral knowledge and often act morally.[9]

The issue I want to address here is whether the naturalistic worldview can *ground* morality, or provide any framework for making moral truth objective. For one thing, we can certainly question whether naturalism can provide moral motivation. The consensus among secular thinkers today seems to be that naturalistic evolution "has granted to us all things that pertain to life and godliness" (to borrow Peter's phrase in 2 Pet. 1:3), only without God.

One of the highest-profile early authors to think about the ramifications for Darwinism and morality was Friedrich Nietzsche. Active as a philosopher in the decades following the release of *On the Origin of Species*, Nietzsche understood the far-reaching

---

9. This is not to say that their actions, even though morally right, can be of any ultimate or salvific value. While they may do what the moral law requires, if they do not do it from faith, it is of no lasting spiritual value: "Whatever does not proceed from faith is sin" (Rom. 14:23). Furthermore, salvation is by *grace* through *faith*, not by works of righteousness (Eph. 2:8–9). The point is merely that they have moral knowledge and sometimes act morally.

significance of evolutionary naturalism, and his full-throated endorsement of its implications sent shock waves through Europe that still reverberate today. Famous for his claim that God is dead, he explained what he saw happening as a result of evolutionary naturalism and the secularism that was replacing a Christian worldview. In one passage, "the madman," who brings the message of God's death, addresses a crowd of onlookers:

> "Where has God gone?" he cried. "I shall tell you. We have killed him—you and I. We are his murderers. But how have we done this? How were we able to drink up the sea? Who gave us the sponge to wipe away the entire horizon? What did we do when we unchained the earth from its sun? Whither is it moving now? Whither are we moving now? Away from all suns? Are we not perpetually falling? Backward, sideward, forward, in all directions? Is there any up or down left? Are we not straying as through an infinite nothing? Do we not feel the breath of empty space? Has it not become colder? Is it not more and more night coming on all the time? Must not lanterns be lit in the morning? Do we not hear anything yet of the noise of the gravediggers who are burying God? Do we not smell anything yet of God's decomposition? Gods too decompose. God is dead. God remains dead. And we have killed him. How shall we, murderers of all murderers, console ourselves?"[10]

Without God, the madman declares that everything is meaningless and adrift in a sea of darkness. He—the madman—is the only one not mad, for he perceives the truth his crowd fails to acknowledge. He knows what follows the death of God, but they cannot or will not see it. Without God, there is no up or down—there is nothing left.

Consider how humans are supposed to have risen to the top of the heap. After all, in any environment we occupy, we take over as

---

10. Friedrich Nietzsche, *The Gay Science*, ed. Walter Kaufmann (New York: Vintage, 1974), 181–82.

the apex species. We dominate our ecosystems. But how do we do that? The consequence of evolution as Nietzsche saw it was that we dominate by out-surviving our rivals in a fierce, deadly competition for resources. Sometimes survival comes easy. Sometimes it's like Clara's lullaby in *Porgy and Bess*:

> Summertime, and the livin' is easy. . . .
> So hush, little baby, don't you cry.[11]

But that is not always the case. Disrupting such easy living are droughts, diseases, food shortages, and natural disasters. When survival pressures mount and it becomes difficult to thrive, adaptations that confer an advantage will ensure that the strong will survive and the weak will disappear.

If evolutionary naturalism is right, there is nothing other than the pressure to survive. As we have seen, adaptations serve that purpose, and that purpose alone. Survival, or what Nietzsche labeled the "will to power," is the only force evolution can exert. The natural question to ask, then, is why anyone or anything would ever try to stop the ascendance of the powerful over the weak. That is the way of nature—why fight it? Why should we be kind or altruistic? Why should we look after our neighbor? Why should we show special care for the weak, the vulnerable, and the elderly? If evolutionary naturalism were true, why should someone behave morally? If someone killed his neighbor, raped his neighbor's wife, and stole all their property, what would be wrong with that from a survival standpoint? Why not be racist or sexist? Why not enslave other people?

I firmly believe these things are all wrong, and so do almost all atheists. The question is, can they say *why* they are wrong? The Christian perspective is that atheists know these things are wrong because God has written his law on their hearts. But what is the naturalist's perspective? According to them, there simply *is* no

---

11. DuBose Heyward and Ira Gershwin, "Summertime," from the score of *Porgy and Bess* (New York: Gershwin Publishing, 1935).

law—there is nothing to write! Everything is morally permissible in service of survival and reproduction. This is Nietzsche's point, and it is hard to see where he goes wrong, given his starting point of evolutionary naturalism.

He was not the only one to make this point either. Many of the most prominent philosophers of the twentieth century agreed with him, especially the existentialists. For instance, one of the leading figures of that intellectual movement, Jean-Paul Sartre, claimed that we are "condemned to be free" and forced to create our own essence by our choices, since there is no God and no transcendent moral law to guide us.[12] This is the frightening outgrowth of understanding humans as merely evolved primates whose creator is the blind, amoral drive to survive and reproduce.

Despite the convincing exposition of these implications in the late nineteenth and early twentieth centuries, the perspective on the moral entailments of evolutionary theory has changed fairly dramatically in the last few decades. Instead of looking at evolution as justifying knavery, the new, kinder and gentler "enlightened" mindset tries to convince us that evolution really just wants us all to love each other. The path humans have taken to success, the argument goes, has been to cooperate, not pant after conquest. It is by extending consideration and genuine altruism to family, friends, and neighbors that humanity thrives. Rather than seeing life as *bellum omnium contra omnes*, or "a perpetuall warre of every man against his neighbour," as Thomas Hobbes put it in the seventeenth century,[13] the trendy view now is to see evolution as making us *nice*.

Is Goodness Good for Us?

Scientifically, this line of argument might develop by noting how "goodness" aids the survival of other species. Treating morality

---

12. Jean-Paul Sartre, *Being and Nothingness*, trans. Hazel E. Barnes (New York: Washington Square Press, 1956), passim.
13. Thomas Hobbes, *Leviathan* (1651).

as an evolutionary puzzle and confining himself to observations of behavior, biologist Douglas Allchin considers everything from honeybees to squirrels to primates. He notes the behaviors they exhibit that promote flourishing, including care for offspring, reciprocal cooperation, and even offering aid to strangers. Many of them display habits that we anthropomorphize as moral, especially when it comes to cooperation versus selfishness. Cooperation is often rewarded; selfishness is often punished. Allchin says:

> Organisms may also actively punish non-cooperators. For example, in a free-ranging (semicaptive) colony of macaques, or rhesus monkeys (*Macaca mulatta*), on an island off Puerto Rico, individuals call to the group when they find food. Individuals that fail to call are frequently discovered and, here, actively punished. They are more likely to be bit, hit, chased or rolled. Cheaters ultimately eat less food. There are costs to deception. . . . Cooperation enforced through punishment yields strong reciprocity. Such punishment has also been observed in the cooperative breeding of fairy wrens and in the shared nesting of paper wasps (*Polistes fuscatus*). . . . In these cases, interactions at the higher, social level regulate behavior, or stimulus-response patterns, at the individual level.[14]

The issue is not merely altruistic behavior, though—it may go deeper than that and involve genuine desire to do good. It is one thing to practice moral behavior; it is another thing to act morally from an inward motivation to do so. As another author states:

> It is quite possible that natural selection would have favored humans who genuinely do care about helping others, i.e., who are capable of "real" or psychological altruism. Suppose there is an evolutionary advantage associated with taking good care of one's children—a quite plausible idea. Then, parents who *really do care* about their children's welfare, i.e., who

---

14. Douglas Allchin, "The Evolution of Morality," *Evolution* 2, no. 4 (2009): 590.

are "real" altruists, will have a higher inclusive fitness, hence
spread more of their genes, than parents who only pretend to
care, or who do not care. Therefore, evolution may well lead
"real" or psychological altruism to evolve.[15]

Evolution, the argument goes, might very well promote good behavior and positive motivations because those things are adaptive; they might support survival and reproduction better than
the alternatives. So the new perspective claims that kindness and
cooperation are the real natural legacy of evolution, not the kind
of selfish or even violent behavior advocated by Nietzsche and
other moral nihilists.

In his provocatively titled book *Value and Virtue in a Godless
Universe*, philosopher Erik Wielenberg seeks to recast morality
in the naturalist mold; he wants to preserve value and morality
without God. That is not to say that he wishes to abandon morality or move beyond good and evil as Nietzsche did, but he tries to
support morality within an atheistic framework.

> In place of [the Christian] vision of oneself as a soldier in a
> war between good and evil, I suggest that naturalists view
> themselves as engaged in a struggle against a wild animal. The
> struggle is not on a battlefield where conflict rages between
> the forces of dark and light and where victory and salvation
> are assured only for the right side. Rather, the struggle is to
> tame an uncaring, irrational beast, and success is anything
> but certain; everyone has something of the beast inside and an
> important part of the struggle is conquering this inner monster.
> The inexorable, uncaring laws of nature are the arena, and
> as much as possible they must be understood and put to use.
> Within the combatants are destructive emotional tendencies
> that arose not as a consequence of the Fall, but rather of the

---

15. Samir Okasha, "Biological Altruism," in *Stanford Encyclopedia of Philosophy*, ed.
Edward N. Zalta (Fall 2013), https://plato.stanford.edu/archives/fall2013/entries/altruism
-biological/.

slow, mindless working of the evolutionary forces that shaped the human mind.[16]

Notice the value-laden language in this passage: "struggle against a wild animal," "an uncaring, irrational beast," "conquering this inner monster," and "destructive emotional tendencies." Wielenberg says that our mission in light of our animality is to fight against it and conquer it. He even advocates a new mission for science: adjusting our brains to be more moral. This, he says, must be the mission of all emerging neuroscience and understanding of the brain. Change the brain, change the person—and the direction of change must be toward moral improvement. After all, he says:

> The source of the heart of darkness—the human nervous system—is part of the natural, physical world; it is not a nonphysical soul, forever inaccessible to science. In a naturalistic world, the human mind is fully a product of blind forces at work over countless eons. There is nothing sacred about its design; it is not part of a divine plan, or a divine construction that we are forbidden to manipulate.[17]

What is this "heart of darkness" he speaks of? In a word, *selfishness*. So, while Wielenberg is less optimistic than some others about how good we are intrinsically, he too reduces the discussion to the brain and nervous-system wiring installed by evolution, enjoining us to amplify the good impulses we have—through science, of course—and tamp down the bad ones. Evolution handed us a mixed bag of good and bad, and we need to choose the good.

At this point (again), my question is simple: Why tame the uncaring, destructive tendencies, as Wielenberg says we must? They can work to serve the purposes of evolution too! Why do we favor some instincts and call them good, such as altruism,

---

16. Erik J. Wielenberg, *Value and Virtue in a Godless Universe* (Cambridge: Cambridge University Press, 2005), 127.

17. Wielenberg, *Value and Virtue in a Godless Universe*, 140–41.

care for family, kindness, self-control, and cooperation? Why do we condemn other instincts, such as violence, anger, rape, and selfishness? Evolution on its own simply does not care and cannot support these moral judgments.

Is Thriving Enough?

In my yard, we have walnut trees in three of the four corners, making us very popular with squirrels. During the fall, the little critters scamper throughout the treetops, often perching somewhere high above the ground with a walnut held in their paws while they nibble through the hard husk. Very often several squirrels occupy the same tree, or nearby ash, spruce, or pine trees. The majority of them are eastern gray squirrels, and for the most part, they do not seem to mind when other squirrels are nearby. Two or three grays can happily share a tree, each one content and at ease. But the gray squirrels are not the only denizens of our little grove: there are also American red squirrels. The peace is immediately broken whenever one of these feisty, aggressive creatures bursts on the scene. Though much smaller than gray squirrels, the red squirrels will chase away the grays, pursuing them from tree to tree to make sure the whole area is cleared of rivals. They will bite if necessary, and make loud unpleasant chattering noises to proclaim their sovereignty over the tree. They are nasty little blighters who do not play well with others.

Which one thrives better? Are gray squirrels more successful, or reds? The answer is *neither*. They are both doing just fine, with a surfeit of each. I would appreciate it if they were maybe thriving a little *less*—that way they would stay out of my boat. But the point is that the "nice" behavior of the gray squirrels and the "mean" behavior of the red squirrels work equally well. Evolution does not and cannot care whether the squirrels are nice or mean; there is no meaningful moral category to appeal to. There is only what works, and it seems that both work equally well. As another philosopher states it:

Suppose morality is what furthers survival. If so, some acts seemingly could be justified, like various examples of genocide. If morality is what furthers survival, why *should* the weak survive? Even more to the point, how do we derive that moral prescription from a description—that the strong in fact tend to survive?[18]

The grays survive by being nice. The reds survive by being mean. That is all that counts from an evolutionary naturalist perspective.

This kind of indifference is obvious throughout Animalia. In a nature show I once watched, a lone wolf was looking for a pack to join. Her mate had died and she was alone and pregnant, unable to hunt effectively by herself and nearing starvation. The documentary recorded her efforts to join another pack, but the pack rejected her—not even allowing her to carry off a bone they had in their cache that had already been stripped of all its meat. She wandered off alone and found a quiet den where she delivered her litter of five pups. When she left the pups in the den to go out to try to find something to eat, the pack that rejected her snuck into the den and ate all five of her pups. She starved to death shortly afterward.

Were the wolves being immoral? Was there something fallen or broken in what happened? The gospel of Jesus Christ declares that the world is groaning under the weight of sin and death. What does evolutionary naturalism declare? Can it say *anything* about that, other than "we don't like it"? What resources does naturalism have to make a judgment that these things *should not* happen—that their occurrence is pointing to something being *wrong*? How can they accuse God of moral malfeasance, of being wicked or culpably indifferent to suffering? As Dawkins has said: "We are survival machines—robot vehicles blindly programmed to preserve the selfish molecules known as genes. . . . We pass away but

---

18. R. Scott Smith, *In Search of Moral Knowledge* (Downers Grove, IL: IVP Academic, 2014), 126.

the genes march on. That is their business. They are the replicators and we are their survival machines. When we have served our purpose we are cast aside."[19] We may disagree with him about the truth of this claim, but it abundantly clear that he correctly sees the implications of his own evolutionary naturalism.

If evolutionary naturalism is true, then nature is valueless. There can be nothing really *right or wrong* with anything people do. Certain behaviors might in fact promote survival better, but whether they do or not, there can be no foundation to appeal to that could help us decide what (if anything) we *ought* to do. There are only inclinations. There are only desires and drives. What we need, but what evolution cannot furnish, are duties and obligations affixed to a firm moral structure. Without a moral foundation, there can be neither goodness nor evil. The naturalists' promises to furnish the grounds of virtue are empty.

19. Richard Dawkins, *The Selfish Gene—40th Anniversary Edition* (Oxford: Oxford University Press, 2016), 44.

10

Reformed Epistemology and the Naturalness of Belief

The nature of knowledge has been the subject of intense philosophical debate for thousands of years. To illustrate some of the complexities, consider a simple thought experiment. If you are like most people, if someone asks whether you believe there is at least one spider in your home, maybe behind a couch or under a bookshelf or hidden in a corner of the basement, or perhaps up in the attic, you will probably say yes. Chances are good, and based on past experience, you believe there is at least one spider somewhere in your home. But suppose someone asks you, once you have admitted that you believe it, if you *know* it. If you do not see one currently, then you might be reluctant to say you *know* there is a spider somewhere in the house even though you *believe* there is.

Knowing something and merely believing it are not the same thing. That is, there are things we believe but would not say we know. Without trying to untangle what those differences might be right now, we may note that we differentiate *having a belief* from *knowing something*. Several candidates might come to mind that set them apart, and earlier in the book we examined one popular but unsuccessful attempt: that knowing something requires scientific, or at least sensory, confirmation.

Consider another example of something you know. Suppose someone asks if you have ever been to the moon. If you are like most people, the answer will be a confident no—there will be no hesitation, no need to plumb the depths of your memory to be sure. If they press you and ask if you are *sure* you have never been to the moon, you will affirm that you know it beyond even the slightest doubt.

The case of the moon belief is a puzzling one as well. Here we seem to have an item of certain knowledge—but what is it based upon? We know that we have not been to the moon because . . . what? We would never claim to remember everything that has happened to us, so we cannot rule it out on those grounds. We do not have any kind of direct empirical evidence that we have always been within a few miles of the earth, like a comprehensive recording of our entire lives that we could scour to see for sure. In addition, we recognize we do not need any evidence like that to have what counts as knowledge. Strangely, in this case the certainty comes from *lacking a memory*. But we would not normally consider a statement to be known by the *absence* of something; we usually say beliefs become knowledge only in the *presence* of something. Again, the point right now is not to say exactly what distinguishes knowledge from mere belief; it is just to note that we are all aware of the difference, and yet saying exactly what it is might be difficult.

Science and Knowledge

Of special prominence today is the approach that says science and science alone can lead to knowledge. This attempt to distinguish belief from knowledge invokes the backing of science as the criterion. In his book *Faith versus Fact*, American geneticist Jerry Coyne exemplifies this attitude. He says:

On the whole, it's difficult to escape the conclusion—based on the paucity of religious scientists, the incessant stream of books using contradictory arguments to promote accommodationism, the constant reassurance by scientific organizations that believers can accept science without violating their faith, and the pervasiveness of creationism in many countries—that there is a problem in harmonizing science and religion, one that worries both sides (but mostly the religious).[1]

Bit by bit, the list of phenomena that once demanded an explanatory God is being whittled down to nothing. Religion's response has been to either reject the science (the tactic of fundamentalists) or bend their theology to accommodate it. But theology can be bent only so far before, by rejecting theological nonnegotiables like the divinity of Jesus, it snaps, turning into nonreligious secular humanism.[2]

I could go on, but the point is clear: religions make explicit claims about reality—about what exists and what happens in the universe. These claims involve the existence of gods . . . how they interact with the world, whether or not there are souls or life after death, and, above all, how the deities wish us to behave. . . . These are empirical claims, and although some may be hard to test, they must, like all claims about reality, be defended with a combination of evidence and reason.[3]

It will not surprise the reader to find that Coyne believes that the claims of religion cannot, despite the best and most sincere efforts of believers, be in harmony with the methods and findings of modern science. But what, according to Coyne, is so special about science and the scientific way of knowing? Science, he says, leads to knowledge because it presents public facts for confirmation. Other fields, such as history or economics, can also lead to

---

1. Jerry A. Coyne, *Faith versus Fact: Why Science and Religion Are Incompatible* (New York: Penguin, 2016), 14.
2. Coyne, *Faith versus Fact*, 16.
3. Coyne, *Faith versus Fact*, 23.

knowledge, but "they do so only to the degree that their methods involve 'science broadly construed.'" Knowledge, he says, is "the public acceptance of facts," and "facts" are statements that can be confirmed *independently* and that result in *consensus*. We can call this the *public confirmation criterion*. To emphasize his point, Coyne says: "Any discipline that studies the universe using the methods of 'broad' science is capable in principle of finding truth and producing knowledge. If it doesn't, no knowledge is possible."[4] Jerry Coyne is merely one example of such an attitude. The current landscape is populated with many prominent figures arguing for the same conclusion.

But is science the only way to knowledge? It seems that we can easily find examples of knowledge that will not meet the public confirmation criterion. For example, I know that this morning I was humming a tune from *Fiddler on the Roof*. If we consider that claim, it will clearly fail to meet the criterion because it is historical, not witnessed by anyone but me, not repeatable, not subject to confirmation or falsification in any way, something I am possibly mistaken about, and so forth. But I have much more confidence in that belief than I do in myriad scientific claims. I am far more convinced that I was humming "Sunrise, Sunset" than that there is isotropic cosmic microwave background radiation or that every creature with a heart also has a kidney. It would be unnecessarily austere to disqualify such beliefs from being knowledge. Even among many claims that could be publicly confirmed in the way suggested above, such confirmation is often impractical or gratuitous. If I believe and know that my wife is a human and not a cleverly designed android, it is *not* because my belief could be publicly confirmed, though in the right circumstances it could. Such confirmation in those cases, even where available, is not necessary for knowledge. These and many other possible examples show that some knowledge claims are perfectly respectable even

---

4. Coyne, *Faith versus Fact*, 186–87.

though they need not or even cannot meet the public confirmation criterion. Saying we know something does not require that it be open to public confirmation.

We must recognize, though, that these examples of knowledge may not speak to the real purpose of the criterion. It is not meant to discount particular beliefs that are specific to a certain time, person, or place. Instead it is meant to address truth claims that speak to the broader structure of reality and apply to entire categories of objects. If we are being as charitable as possible to the public confirmation criterion, it seems we should limit its intended application to propositions that purport to apply to categories of objects or events. After all, my belief about what I was humming is not a belief about memories in general; my belief about my wife is not a belief about all humans. The criterion is intended to transcend such particulars and make claims about entire classes. The difficulty here is how to state that requirement without it collapsing into a tautology. If we refine it to say that only scientific knowledge needs to meet the public confirmation criterion, that would fail to rule out religious knowledge as its advocates seek to do. That definition would be too narrow for their purposes. If we say beliefs count as knowledge only if they are about publicly confirmable propositions, we fail to include ordinary items of knowledge (like the examples above) as we ought to. That definition would then be too broad. It is not at all clear how to make the criterion wide enough to include everything it should but narrow enough not exclude anything it should not—a very delicate balancing act to pull off without collapsing into mere special pleading for the uniqueness and superiority of a scientific way of knowing.

Knowledge of God

So it seems that science is not the only way to knowledge. Of special interest for us, however, is how everything we have talked about throughout this book—science, souls, freedom, morality, the religious propensity, religious experience, neuroscience, and cognitive science in general—bears on one particular epistemological question: the knowledge of God. In particular, how should we think about the knowledge of God in a way that is faithful to the Scriptures but also informed by our previous reflections? There may not be a single definitive answer, but there is at least one promising route we can explore.

Before we do, it would help to see some of the things Scripture has to say about the knowledge of God. In 1 John 5:13, the apostle says, "I write these things to you who believe in the name of the Son of God, that you may know that you have eternal life." We *believe*, but we also *know*. In fact, that chapter contains quite a list of things John says we can know regarding the Christian faith: we know that when we love and obey God, we will also love other believers (5:2); we know God hears our prayers and answers them (5:15); we know that being born of God leads to holiness (5:18); we know that we are from God and the world is under the power of the evil one (5:19); and "we know that the Son of God has come and has given us understanding, so that we may know him who is true" (5:20). All of those knowledge claims—most impressively that the Son of God has come to show us the Father, and that by believing we can know we have eternal life—are packed into that one single chapter.

Another place to see very clearly how the New Testament authors thought about the knowledge of God is found in Paul's letter to the Romans. Especially in the first chapter, we see Paul affirming the universal nature of the knowledge of God, and how the truth of God's existence and character is not only accessible to all people but also a part of what it is natural to believe. Paul says:

> For the wrath of God is revealed from heaven against all ungodliness and unrighteousness of men, who by their unrighteousness suppress the truth. For what can be known about God is plain to them, because God has shown it to them. For his invisible attributes, namely, his eternal power and divine

nature, have been clearly perceived, ever since the creation of the world, in the things that have been made. So they are without excuse. For although they knew God, they did not honor him as God or give thanks to him, but they became futile in their thinking, and their foolish hearts were darkened. Claiming to be wise, they became fools. (Rom. 1:18–22)

There are undoubtedly other things happening in this passage too as Paul builds his case that all people—Jews and Gentiles alike—have fallen into sin and are in need of salvation. However, he clearly affirms here what I have been calling the naturalness of religious belief. The thing that leads to unbelief, Paul suggests here, is not a lack of evidence or the inclination to believe but rather the active suppression of the truth because of an aversion to the righteousness God calls us to.

A similar sentiment is expressed in one of King David's most eloquent songs, Psalm 19:

The heavens proclaim the glory of God.
The skies display his craftsmanship.
Day after day they continue to speak;
night after night they make him known.
They speak without a sound or word;
their voice is never heard.
Yet their message has gone throughout the earth,
and their words to all the world. (vv. 1–4 NLT)

The idea that God can be known to some extent by all people at all times is called "general revelation." That is, as opposed to the "special revelation" of himself through Scripture and the life of Jesus Christ, God has revealed himself generally through both external means (such as nature) and internal means (such as human conscience). Says one theologian:

The view that God has revealed himself through what he has made is as old as Genesis, interpreted through the poetry of the Psalms, widely attested in the prophets, confirmed by Jesus and the apostles, with the vision of the whole earth finally having its tongue loosed to sing God's praise. There is a divinely appointed order in creation that can be appealed to even in special revelation. . . . God is said to reveal himself in the thunder and lightning, as in the natural processes of planting and harvest, in his command over the winds and the seas and the sun, moon, and stars, and in his care for his creatures. . . . Everyone is aware of God's existence, even of his moral will.[5]

John Calvin, the sixteenth-century French theologian and Reformer, insisted that we have the ability to know God, and that this ability is a part of our noetic scaffolding. Says Calvin: "There is within the human mind, and indeed by natural instinct, an awareness of divinity. This we take to be beyond controversy. To prevent anyone from taking refuge in the pretense of ignorance, God himself has implanted in all men a certain understanding of his divine majesty."[6] Where belief is absent, it is because the knowledge of God is "smothered or corrupted, partly by ignorance, partly by malice."[7] Vanity, pride, deception and blindness of parents and teachers, neglect and indifference to the truth, the pain of guilt, the love of sin, and many other causes lead to the seed of knowledge failing to ripen, much less bear fruit.[8]

Building on the thought of Calvin was another Reformed theologian, Herman Bavinck. He argued that science can give us a certain kind of knowledge but is inadequate for the tasks of living and certainly unable to fill our hearts or satisfy our longings. For that, Bavinck said, we needed the "certainty of faith" that comes with trusting and knowing Christ.[9] Cornelius Van Til, in turn,

---

5. Michael Horton, *The Christian Faith: A Systematic Theology for Pilgrims on the Way* (Grand Rapids, MI: Zondervan, 2011), 140–41.

6. John Calvin, *Institutes of the Christian Religion*, ed. John T. McNeill, trans. Ford Lewis Battles (Philadelphia: Westminster, 1960), 1.3.1.

7. Calvin, *Institutes*, 1.4.

8. Calvin, *Institutes*, 1.4.1.

9. See, for example, chap. 2 of his *The Certainty of Faith* (St. Catherines, ON: Paideia, 1980).

insisted that the Reformed perspective on knowledge takes the existence of God and the lordship of Jesus Christ as presuppositions; they together are the starting point of knowledge, not the conclusion of an argument.

In the late twentieth century, philosopher William Alston picked up a similar thread. He likened beliefs about God—especially beliefs that guide our actions and attitudes—to sensory beliefs such as that there is a cup in front of me. There is no way to prove on independent grounds that our sensory perceptions are veridical (that is, that they tell the truth about the world around us), but it is rational to believe and act on them anyway. In the same way, people who believe and act on religious beliefs may also be justified, especially when those beliefs arise from personal experiences.[10] Robert Audi, another contemporary philosopher, agrees with this approach, "since it grounds the justification of some very important religious beliefs in experience rather than in evidential beliefs or direct rational apprehension" in the same way that other beliefs based on experience can acquire justification.[11]

Reformed Epistemology

Countless philosophers and theologians agree with this general approach to religious belief and knowledge. Many advocates of it present somewhat competing perspectives, but perhaps none has done more than Alvin Plantinga to expound, popularize, and persuasively present what is now commonly called "Reformed epistemology." Plantinga is possibly the best known and most respected living Christian philosopher, and he has extensively, systematically defended the claim that belief in God can be fully warranted and constitute knowledge.

---

10. For starters, see William P. Alston, "Religious Experience and Religious Belief," *Noûs* 16, no. 1 (1982): 3–12, and especially his book *Perceiving God: The Epistemology of Religious Experience* (Ithaca, NY: Cornell University Press, 1991).

11. Robert Audi, *Epistemology* (New York: Routledge, 2011), 321.

Essential to Plantinga's defense of Reformed epistemology is his criticism of foundationalism, especially in its modern and classical manifestations. The kind of foundationalist approach to knowledge in Plantinga's sights is that which insists that only self-evident beliefs, beliefs that are evident to the senses, or beliefs that are incorrigible can serve as properly basic. A self-evident belief is one for which the truth value is obvious once the terms are understood. That a triangle is three-sided and a bachelor is un-married are self-evident, as is the claim that a collection of eleven oranges has more elements than a collection of four oranges. A be-lief evident to the senses is one that has been derived from seeing, touching, hearing, smelling, or tasting something. An incorrigible belief is one that cannot be corrected by anyone else. If I believe I am thinking of a horse, then I *am* thinking of a horse—no one can tell me otherwise. If I think I am in pain, then I am in pain, even if a team of crack physicians runs every diagnostic test on me imaginable and cannot find anything wrong. No one can tell me I am not in pain; that belief cannot be corrected by someone else. The foundationalist under consideration says that only such beliefs—or beliefs logically entailed by such beliefs—can truly count as knowledge.

The notions of *basic* and *properly basic* are also key in this ac-count. A basic belief is one that is not derived, deduced, or inferred from another belief. Immediate sensory beliefs are of this variety, as are many others. My belief that my back aches is basic. If I look at my hand, I perceive and believe immediately that it is a hand and not a flipper. That is also basic. If my dog enters the room, I know without thinking about it that it is Homer and not a bear or a rooster; that is also a basic belief. I know I had peanut butter on toast for breakfast as soon as I conjure up the memory—no argu-ment is required and no inferences are made. So my memory of having breakfast is basic too.

What these have in common is that they are not held at the end of a chain of reasoning or a lengthy string of inferences. No argument is needed, and usually none is even available for them. A *properly* basic belief, then, is a basic belief of a special kind—namely, one that we are within our epistemic rights to hold. For beliefs to be considered proper, we only need to assume these beliefs do not result from hallucinations, faulty memory, malfunctioning faculties, or any other problematic source. Unlike some other beliefs, properly basic beliefs deserve the confidence we have in them. Assenting to them is proper.

So much for definitional preliminaries. When it comes to the foundationalist and evidentialist challenges to religious belief, Plantinga argues that much of the problem lies with putting the epistemological cart before the horse. Consider, for example, the criteria of the kind of foundationalism we have in mind— a kind of foundationalism that rejects religious knowledge on the grounds that it fails to satisfy the criteria for knowledge. According to the classic foundationalist, a belief counts as knowledge only if it is self-evident, incorrigible, or evident to the senses, or is entailed by beliefs that are self-evident, sensory, or incorrigible (we can label these SESI beliefs). If something does not fit into those categories, it does not meet the strict requirements for knowledge.

But immediately a problem emerges for foundationalism, for the foundationalist claim itself is not self-evident, evident to the senses, or incorrigible; nor is it logically entailed by beliefs that are. In other words, the proposition *only SESI beliefs constitute knowledge* is itself not self-evident (it is not seen to be true simply by understanding the terms), incorrigible (it is not the sort of thing one could not possibly be wrong about), or evident to the senses (it is not a report of a visual, auditory, tactile, olfactory, or taste sensation). Since it fails to fall into one of those categories, it also fails to qualify as something we can know. Thus, it fails to meet its own criteria. The SESI restriction on knowledge is self-defeating. It crashes to the ground after cutting off the branch it was sitting on. Plantinga describes the problem well:

What is the status of the criteria for knowledge, or proper basicality, or justified belief? Typically, these are universal statements. The modern foundationalist's criterion for proper basicality, for example, is doubly universal:

> For any proposition *A* and person *S*, *A* is properly basic for *S* if and only if *A* is incorrigible for *S* or self-evident to *S*.

But how could one know a thing like that? What are its credentials? Clearly enough, [this criterion] isn't self-evident or just obviously true. But if it isn't, how does one arrive at it? ... [The criterion] itself is neither self-evident nor incorrigible; hence in accepting [it] as basic, the modern foundationalist violates the condition of proper basicality he himself lays down in accepting it.[12]

In light of this problem, Plantinga asks a pointed, powerful question that we should all ask whenever an argument like the foundationalist one is presented: "Why should we believe [it], or pay it any attention?"[13] This kind of argument is meant to show us that belief in God cannot be properly basic. But it fails spectacularly, and we should all practice pointing this out.

In fact, this same problem plagues many approaches to epistemology—including all of the ones we have surveyed that are hostile to religious belief. Advocates of Reformed epistemology emphasize the problem with such top-down approaches. Such approaches espouse criteria that must be met for any belief to count as knowledge, but the criteria themselves almost never meet their own standards (e.g., that all knowledge is from the senses is not itself from the senses). Even if they do, they typically eliminate all kinds of perfectly acceptable and obvious forms of knowledge (e.g., the "public confirmation criterion" we discussed earlier rules

---

12. Alvin Plantinga, "Is Belief in God Properly Basic?," *Noûs* 15, no. 1 (1981): 41–51, quoting 49.
13. Plantinga, "Is Belief in God Properly Basic?," 49.

out knowledge of our own minds). But regardless of whether they succeed in dodging those bullets, there is a deeper problem. Again, Plantinga puts it well:

> The fact is that [no] revealing necessary and sufficient condition for proper basicality follows from clearly self-evident premises by clearly acceptable arguments. And hence the proper way to arrive at such a criterion is, broadly speaking, *inductive*. We must assemble examples of beliefs and conditions such that the former are obviously properly basic in the latter. We must then frame hypotheses as to the necessary and sufficient conditions for proper basicality and test these hypotheses by reference to those examples. . . . Accordingly, criteria for proper basicality must be reached from below rather than from above; they should not be presented as *ex Cathedra*, but argued to and tested by a relevant set of examples.[14]

It is in this sense that Reformed epistemology thinks many other approaches put the cart before the horse. Instead of looking up into the sky and pulling down the criteria for knowledge as if they were handed down as to Moses on Mount Sinai, we should construct a working definition of knowledge and its origins out of an examination of what we know. We take examples of things we know—we know that we have bodies, that we are more than two minutes old, that other people also have minds, that bread nourishes us but gravel doesn't, that 2+3=5, that we cannot fly around the room by flapping our arms, and so on—and we think about how we formed those beliefs and what makes them justified.

Surely these examples of things we know are uncontroversial. But should we expect them all to be? Should we expect, when we reflect on what will happen when we undertake this investigation, that all reasonable people will have exactly the same list of examples to start with? That, it seems, would be too much

---

14. Plantinga, "Is Belief in God Properly Basic?," 49–50.

to hope for. Indeed, when we consider the wide range of beliefs and life experiences, we would positively expect to have quite a number of disagreements. In that case, what should we do? How should we handle the disagreement with others who question our examples? In short, Plantinga's advice is not to worry about it. He explains:

> But there is no reason to assume, in advance, that everyone will agree on the examples. The Christian will of course suppose that belief in God is entirely proper and rational; if he doesn't accept this belief on the basis of other propositions, he will conclude that it is basic for him, and quite properly so. Followers of Bertrand Russell and Madelyn Murray O'Hare may disagree, but how is that relevant? Must my criteria, or those of the Christian community, conform to their examples? Surely not. The Christian community is responsible to *its* set of examples, not to theirs.[15]

Reformed epistemology is a form of *reliabilism* in epistemology. In the history of discussions about the nature of knowledge going back at least to Plato, there has been general agreement about what is required for knowledge: when we have knowledge, we have a justified true belief in something. This is a major oversimplification, but what it presents to us is useful. To know something, a person must first believe it. This gets at my earlier point that knowledge is a special kind of belief. Second, the belief must be true—nobody can know something false. The Vikings did not know the world was shaped like a shield resting on the roots of the world tree, Yggdrasil. They believed it, but they did not know it, because it was not true.

The last element points out that randomly held beliefs do not count as knowledge, even if they turn out to be true. To know

---

15. Alvin Plantinga, "Religious Belief without Evidence," in *Religious Experience and Religious Belief: Essays in the Epistemology of Religion*, ed. Joseph Runzo and Craig K. Ihara (New York: University Press of America, 1986), 174.

something, there must be some kind of justification, warrant, or authority to the belief. The idea with reliabilism is that a true belief moves up a bracket into the realm of knowledge when the belief is the result of reliable processes.[16] In Plantinga's work, the belief would result from properly functioning cognitive faculties operating in the environment they were designed for. There is a lot in there calling for elaboration, but for now it is enough for us to think a little about which cognitive faculties we have and what counts as proper function. Though space precludes a full defense of it here, the notion is that the Bible presents us with an account of human nature according to which one of our faculties is what is often called the *sensus divinitatis*. Like our other senses, it is a sort of detector that, when functioning properly and in the right situations, will form properly basic true beliefs in us about God. It isn't always in the right kind of setting to be activated, and it isn't always functioning properly in everyone, but the *sensus divinitatis* can be a reliable source of knowledge.

> If Christian belief is true as, naturally enough, the Christian will think, it will be in view of enabling us to see the truth of "the great things of the Gospel" (as Jonathan Edwards calls them). She will no doubt think that these processes essentially involve what Calvin calls "the internal witness (or testimony) of the Holy Spirit" and what Aquinas calls "the internal instigation of the Holy Spirit." And, of course, these processes will then be truth-aimed: they are aimed at enabling us to form these true beliefs about what God has done and about the way of salvation.[17]

---

16. Philosophers reading this may be howling by now. I am using "justified true belief" without mentioning the Gettier problem; I am using warrant (externalist) and justification (internalist) interchangeably; I introduced the problem of the criterion without mentioning Roderick Chisholm; I treat process reliabilism as the only form while ignoring agent and virtue reliabilism; I am not saying anything at all about what counts as a belief, or specifying a theory of truth, etc. Let them howl, those things are just not important here.

17. Alvin Plantinga, "Games Scientists Play," in *The Believing Primate: Scientific, Philosophical, and Theological Reflections on the Origin of Religion*, ed. Jeffrey Schloss and Michael Murray (Oxford: Oxford University Press: 2009), 148.

Made to Know God

The way to approach the question of belief in God, then, is to affirm with confidence what the Scriptures teach: we are meant to know God, and our knowledge of him is in no way epistemologically disrespectable. The complaint that it fails to meet the strictures of this or that set of criteria is not something to worry about, since those criteria usually don't even meet their *own* standards; in addition, they rule out a lot of commonsense knowledge that should be acceptable. Moreover, starting with criteria is probably the wrong way to begin anyway. Instead, we build our view of knowledge from the ground up, starting with examples of what we know and seeing what our warranted true beliefs have in common. Using this method and noting the problems with the other approaches, we can safely conclude there is no reason to exclude belief in God as being properly basic. We can instead confidently embrace it as the product of a regenerated mind, the mind of Christ. Pastor and philosopher Greg Bahnsen expressed it this way:

> If the Christian will evidence commitment to Christ's personal Lordship and presuppose the word of the Lord, then he will be walking in Christ after the manner in which he received Him. Hereby you will be "rooted in Him" rather than rooted in the apostate presuppositions of worldly philosophy. . . . Such firm, presuppositional faith in Christ will resist the secular world's demand for neutrality and reject the unbeliever's standards of knowledge and truth in favor of the authority of Christ's word.[18]

Armed with this understanding, we can look back and ask whether the Reformed approach comports with what we have seen from cognitive science about the naturalness of religious belief. While many from the scientific community think religious

---

18. Greg Bahnsen, *Always Ready: Directions for Defending the Faith* (Texarkana, AR: Covenant Media, 1996), 16–17.

knowledge is debunked by their findings, not everyone agrees. It is not only philosophers and theologians who think that the science fits with the view of human nature and knowledge I have described from Scripture. We can question the methodology and assumptions behind much of the science, as I have done, and conclude with many researchers who allege there are systematic problems with methodology and research practice that undermine the studies. The hypothesis that religious beliefs are a natural reaction to features "hardwired" in our brains fits well with everything else we know. Are they compatible with a naturalistic evolutionary framework too? With some reservations, as we have seen, the answer is yes.

But are they also compatible with a Christian view of human nature? The answer again seems to be yes. Whether we take them as supportive or hostile to Christianity is largely a function of our presuppositions, not the science itself. As philosopher Myron Penner observes when discussing whether cognitive science of religion (CSR) provides aid and comfort to atheism:

> CSR, it turns out, does not provide evidence for atheism. It provides no religiously-neutral empirical support for atheism such that CSR is more probable on atheism than on theism. Atheism neither best explains CSR, nor is CSR the kind of observation we should find surprising if theism is true. . . . However, and this is a key point often overlooked by atheists who seek to use CSR in service of atheism, this "aid and comfort" only arises if one already is an atheist. CSR fits with certain things that atheists hold to be true and/or desire to be true—that should provide some comfort. However, CSR also fits with certain things that theists hold to be true and/or desire to be true.[19]

The findings from some researchers openly affirm that our unique human ability to (at least apparently) be in contact with

---

19. Myron A. Penner, "Cognitive Science of Religion, Atheism, and Theism," *Faith and Philosophy* 35, no. 1 (2018): 123–24.

God and form beliefs about divine and supernatural beings provides some evidence that there may be truth behind those beliefs. One might certainly think these findings provide at least prima facie evidence that a transcendent realm exists in the same way that our other beliefs—visual, auditory, and the rest—provide initial evidence to believe in the objects they report to encounter (trees, barking dogs, etc.).

It is possible that the cognitive faculties which tend to produce religious beliefs are malfunctioning, that they are unwarranted but emerged in human history purely for their adaptive value. But why should we believe that rather than believing the Christian account developed here? In general, the answer will display more of a commitment to a worldview than a sound argument. But worldviews themselves—whether atheistic, scientistic, Marxist, postmodern, skeptical, or whatever—are also the product of cognitive faculties which, according to those worldviews, were developed *not* because they produced true beliefs but merely because they produced beliefs that helped us adapt to our environment. In other words, if we reject Christian or other supernatural beliefs on the grounds that such beliefs were never aimed at truth but only aided survival, then why would atheistic or skeptical beliefs be exempt from similar scrutiny? The kinds of belief needed for survival are fairly low-level: Can I eat that? Will that eat me? How do I warm up? How can I save this food for later? Presumably Christians and skeptics are in pretty similar circumstances there.

But both Christians and non-Christians have beliefs about issues related to meaning and value, the nature of knowledge, the origin of the cosmos, the meaning of life, the existence of God—subjects that seem very far removed from daily survival questions. So, when skeptics or atheists adopt a worldview according to which there is no God (and all the entailments that go with such a belief), they are doing so by relying on their cognitive faculties and belief-forming mechanisms, but they have already said those powers are aimed only at survival, not truth. If that is the case, why should the atheist trust the faculties to show them the truth of atheism but question those same faculties when someone else claims they support belief in God? If neuroscience were understood as undercutting *religious* belief by undermining our confidence in the deliberations of our cognitive faculties, it would also undercut *irreligious* belief for all the same reasons. As one team of neuroscience researchers concluded when reviewing, summarizing, and critiquing recent work in cognitive science:

> It should be noted that other convictions and beliefs (be they atheistic, agnostic, or for example political) also emerge from the same cognitive faculties that some consider not to be aimed at producing true beliefs but to merely subserve adaptation to the environment. . . . Thus, we would highlight that the theories and the neuroscientific findings we discussed in no way provide a defeater for religious beliefs. . . . Neuroscientific findings can be integrated in both a theistic as well as an atheistic worldview but these views are not entailed by the empirical evidence itself.[20]

It seems, then, that religious believers are acting perfectly within their epistemic rights and at least potentially meeting the requirements of knowledge when they believe in God and affirm, along with Saint Paul, that "God our Savior . . . desires all people to be saved and to come to the knowledge of the truth" (1 Tim. 2:3–4).

20. Michiel van Elk and André Aleman, "Brain Mechanisms in Religion and Spirituality: An Integrative Predictive Processing Framework," *Neuroscience and Biobehavioral Reviews* 73 (2017): 359–78, quoting 374.

General Index

absolute unitary being, 88, 92
adaptationists (religious beliefs), 77, 80
Allchin, Douglas, 174
Alston, William, 189
altruism, in naturalistic evolution, 172–73, 174, 176
amygdala, 89
animality, fighting against, 175–76
animal life, 103
animal suffering, 178
anthropology, 14, 23
Aristotle, 30–32
Arminianism, 143, 151
Arminius, Jacobus, 155
Aspect, Alain, 146
atheism, 55, 169, 172, 197, 199
Atran, Scott, 67, 69
Audi, Robert, 189
Augustine, 110, 143, 152–53

Bacon, Francis, 33, 37, 55
Bahnsen, Greg, 196
Barbour, Ian, 54
Barrett, Justin, 66, 68–69
Barth, Karl, 48
basic beliefs, 190–91
Bavinck, Herman, 188
belief(s)
  justification of, 189
  evident to senses, 190
  and knowledge, 181, 186
  as properly basic, 196
  undermined by naturalistic evolution, 167–69
Bell's theorem, 128, 146

Bible. *See* Scripture
"biomechanical puppets," 144
Bishop, John, 157
Blackwell, Richard J., 30–31
"blind faith," 166
body-soul dualism, 16–18, 107, 109–10, 132–33, 138
  arguments against, 113–15, 120
  of Descartes, 112
  and libertarian freedom, 156
body-soul union, 22–23
Bohr, Niels, 136
Boyer, Pascal, 71–76
Boyle, Robert, 33, 57
Brahe, Tycho, 31
brain chemistry, 131
brain states and mental states, 130
Brentano, Franz, 70
Butler, Joseph, 110

Calvin, John, 57–58, 143, 152–53, 188
Calvinism, 143, 150–53
Carpenter, W. B., 58
causal likeness principle, 122
causation, 124–29
"certainty of faith," 188
Chalcedonian Definition, 22
Chalmers, David, 115
Chesterton, G. K., 62–63
Chisholm, Roderick, 157, 195n16
Christian anthropology, 14, 15–16
Christology, and anthropology, 23
chronological snobbery, 110
Clark, James Kelly, 117

Clifford, William, 51
cognitive processes, unreliability of, 81
cognitive science, 14, 24
cognitive science of religion (CSR),
    66–72, 78–79, 161, 165, 197
Collins, Robin, 55, 128
comfort
    in the afterlife, 78
    from religion, 73
compatibilism, 141, 143–46, 158–59
    and Christianity, 150–55
concurrence, 60, 119
consciousness, 56
    "easy problems" of, 115
    "hard problem" of, 115–17, 137
consequence argument, 144
conservation of energy, 122–24, 129
cooperation versus selfishness, 174–77
Copernicus, 30–31
correlations, 130
cosmological argument, 51, 55
counterfactual freedom, 125, 142, 157
counterintuitive ideas, 67–70
Coyne, Jerry, 182–84
Craig, William Lane, 55
creationists, 39–40

Dallinger, W. H., 58
Damasio, Antonio, 89–90
Darwin, Charles, 36–38, 42, 45, 168
data
    and background beliefs, 43
    explanation of, 42–43
Dawkins, Richard, 37, 39–40, 51, 166,
    178–79
decision-making, 146–50
deduction, 163–64
deism, 35
delusion, 97
Dennett, Daniel, 70, 79–80
Descartes, René, 33, 57, 108, 110,
    111–12, 138–40, 166
determinism, 144–46
DeWeese, Garrett, 164
diachronic determinism, 145
Dirckx, Sharon, 98–99
discomfort, from religious belief, 73
divine action, compatible with laws of
    nature, 119–20

divine sovereignty and human responsi-
    bility, 141
DNA, 103–4
"doctrine of souls," 113
dorsolateral prefrontal cortex (dlPFC),
    90–91, 148
Draper, John William, 37
dreams, 96–98, 100
Drummond, Henry, 38
dualism. *See* body-soul dualism
Duhem-Quine thesis, 43

Eagleton, Terry, 42
Eastern philosophy, 88
EEG (electroencephalogram), 86, 97,
    146
Effingham, Nikk, 114
emergentism, 149
empirical observations, theological
    ramifications of, 54
empirical verifiability, 50
encounters with God, 83–84, 98, 101
    in Scripture, 93–96
energy conservation, 127–29
Epicureanism, 33
epistemic rights, 191
Erickson, Millard, 155
Evans, Stephen, 139–40
evidence, in science, 51–52
evolution, 15, 36–39, 57
    can appeal to no moral category,
    177–78
evolutionary morality, 14
evolutionary naturalism, as valueless, 179
evolutionary psychology, 14, 24, 81
Executive Inhibition Hypothesis, 90
existentialism, 173
experts, 49–50

facts, 49–50, 184
faith, definition of, 51–53
faith and fact, 48–49, 51, 54
fall, 20
fine-tuning, 55
fMRI (functional magnetic resonance
    imaging), 147, 148
forgiveness of sins, 21
foundationalism, 190, 191
Franklin, Benjamin, 57

freedom, 15, 24, 33, 141–43, 149, 153, 156–59
Freud, Sigmund, 78
frontal lobes, 88
fruit of the Holy Spirit, 101
fundamentalists, 183

Galen, 137
Galileo, 29–32, 42, 43, 57, 61, 108
Gassendi, Pierre, 33, 57
general relativity, 127–29
general revelation, 187–88
geocentricism, 29–32
"ghost in the machine," 108
God
    actions of, 58–63
    as Creator, 63
    immanence of, 59
    presence of, 83
    sovereignty of, 141, 143
    as watchmaker, 36
"God helmet," 92
"god-of-the-gaps" arguments, 36, 39–42, 61, 107
goodness, 173
Gould, Stephen Jay, 48, 49, 53
gravity, 127
Gray, Asa, 58
Greek philosophy, 110–11

Harris, Sam, 144, 146–47, 149
heliocentrism, 28–32, 37
Herophilus, 137
Hobbes, Thomas, 33, 173
Hodge, Charles, 58
human hearts, seek comfort, 73
human intellect, illusion-prone, 75–77
human minds, demand explanation, 72
human nature, 14, 15–20
    and the gospel, 20–23
    material accounts of, 114
    uniqueness of, 104
humans and apes, genetic and brain similarities, 105
human society, requires order, 73–75
Hume, David, 125
Huygens, Christiaan, 61–62
hyperactive agency detection devices (HADDs), 79–80

ideal gas law, 50
illusion of religion, 75–77
image of Christ, 101
image of God, 14, 15, 18, 104, 170
incorrigible beliefs, 190
indeterminism, 56, 146
individualism, 88
induction, 53, 163–65, 193
influence systems, 72
inhibition, 91
Intelligent Design, 39, 55, 162
intentional stance, 70–71
interaction (mind-body), 121–29
irreducibly complex systems, 55
irresistible grace, 153n11
Isaiah, encounter with God, 93–94
Islam, 42, 75

Jacobs, Jonathan D., 156
Jeeves, Malcolm, 107
Jesus Christ
    natures of, 22–23
    reliability of, 21–22
    transfiguration of, 16–17
John, encounter with God in Patmos, 94–95
Johnson, Samuel, 142–43, 156
Judaism, 42
justified true belief, 194–95

kalam version of cosmological argument, 55
Kekes, John, 165
Kepler, Johannes, 57
Kim, Jaegwon, 149
Kingsley, Charles, 38
knowing God, 18–19, 185–89, 196–99
knowledge, versus mere belief, 181

Laplace, Pierre-Simon, 34
laws of nature, and divine action, 119–20
Lewis, C. S., 24–25, 41, 63, 110, 153–54, 168–69
libertarianism, 141–43, 144, 149, 155–57
Libet, Benjamin, 146
life after death, 21
limbic system, 88, 89

Lindberg, David, 32
Livingstone, David, 38
Locke, John, 33
Luther, Martin, 143, 152–53

Madueme, Hans, 18
Marx, Karl, 78
material determinism, 146–47
materialism, 15, 24, 145–46
    and compatibilism, 150
    and libertarianism, 156
    undermines reason, 168–69
Mather, Cotton, 57
McLean v. Arkansas Board of Educa-
    tion, 162–63
mechanism, 33–36, 37
mechanisms, and consciousness, 115–16
meditation, 96
meditative practices, 84–85
memory, 182
mental and physical, 115–17
mental causation, 150
mere conservationism, 59–60
metaphysical materialism, 106
Miller, William, 38
mind, as *tabula rasa*, 33
mind-body dualism. *See* body-soul
    dualism
mind-body interaction, 121–29
minded agents, 70–71
minimally counterintuitive ideas (MCI),
    68–69, 70, 76, 79–80
modus tollens, 43
Moore, Aubrey, 38
moral argument (for theism), 51
morality
    humanity "wired" for, 19–20
    undermined by naturalistic evolution,
        169–73
    without God, 175–76
Moreland, J. P., 56, 145, 156–57, 158,
    164
Morris, Francis Orpen, 38
MRI (magnetic resonance imagining),
    86
Murphy, Nancey, 56
Muslims, coming to faith in Christ in
    dreams, 96
mystical experience, 87–88, 91, 99

naturalism, 15
    and minds, 158
    unverified foundations of, 165–69
naturalistic evolution, 19
    survival in, 178–79
    undermines beliefs, 165–69
    undermines morality, 169–73
natural laws, 35, 36, 61, 162–63
natural philosophers, 33
natural theology, 54–56
neural activity, and religious behavior,
    85–87
neurophysiology, 14, 20
neuroscience
    questionable claims of, 24
    undermines religious and irreligious
        belief, 199
neurotransmitters, 89
Newberg, Andrew, 85–86, 88–89
Newton, Isaac, 33–36, 42, 50, 57, 61,
    62, 108
Nietzsche, Friedrich, 78, 170–72, 175
nihilism, 175
non-adaptationists (religious beliefs),
    77–80
nonoverlapping magisteria (NOMA),
    48, 53–54
nonreductive physicalism, 149

objective probability, 133–34
observability, 162
occasionalism, 60, 119
Ockham's razor, 114
ontological argument, 51
ordinary religious experience, 99–102
original sin, 33
Overton, William, 162–63, 164

Paley, William, 36
pareidolia, 79
parsimony in ontology, 114
Pascal, Blaise, 57
Paul
    encounter with God, 95
    on the soul, 17
Peacocke, Arthur, 56
Pelagius, 143, 155
Penner, Myron, 197
Penrose, Roger, 127–28

Pereboom, Derk, 145
Persinger, Michael, 91–93
PET scan (positron-emission tomography), 86
philosophers of science, 43, 50
philosophical anthropology, 14
phrenological trap, 89–90
physicalism, 114, 133, 144, 149, 156, 159
Plantinga, Alvin, 56, 167–68, 189–95
Plato, 110, 112, 117
plum pudding model of the atom, 44–45
Polkinghorne, John, 56, 129
ponto-geniculo-occipital (PGO) waves, 97
Popper, Karl, 50
Porgy and Bess (opera), 172
potter-clay analogy, 152
power, 78
"powers" view (causation), 125
prefontal cortex (PFC), 88, 104–5
presupposition, knowledge of God as, 189
probabilistic view (causation), 125
probability, 133–35, 164
problem of other minds, 70
"progress of science" argument (PSA), 106–8, 113–14, 120, 121
properly basic beliefs, 190–91, 193
property dualism, 149
providence, 57
pseudoscience, 162
psychological altruism, 174–75
Ptolemy, 30–32, 61
public confirmation criterion, 184–85, 192

quantum mechanics, 56, 127, 128–29, 136, 146, 167

rational soul, 111
reason, undermined by materialism, 168–69
Reformed epistemology, 69, 189–95
Reid, Thomas, 110
"relata of causation," 125
reliabilism, 194–95
religion
    accommodation to science, 183
    comfort from, 73
    explanation from, 72
    harmony with science, 183
    as influence on brain, 72
    as prescientific ignorance, 27–28, 45
    rejection of science, 183
religious belief
    as by-product of evolution, 15, 19
    as cognitive illusion, 75
    hardwired in human brains, 197
    naturalness of, 187
    order from, 73–74
    orgins of, 66
    persistence of, 65–66
religious experience, 84–87, 89, 91
    in the Bible, 93–96
    as encounter with God, 83–85
    as mere brain waves, 84, 99
    ordinary, 99–102
religious propensity, 19, 41, 71–77, 80, 185
REM (rapid eye movement) stage of sleep, 97
Reppert, Victor, 56
ritual, 74–75
Robinson, Daniel, 109, 137–38
Russell, Robert, 56
Rutherford, Ernest, 44
Ryle, Gilbert, 108–9

Sartre, Jean-Paul, 173
science
    conflict with naturalism, 167–68
    based on evidence, 51–52
    as observable, 162
    as only way to knowledge, 182–85
    presuppositions of, 165
    provides certain kind of knowledge, 188
    surprises in, 135–36
    trust in, 161–65
science denier, 109–10
science and religion
    conflict between, 28, 31, 32, 37, 42–45, 47
    as partners, 54–58
    as strangers, 47–54
scientific anthropology, 113
scientific hypotheses, 43–45, 164

scientific usefulness, as criterion of
    belief, 118–19
Scripture
    encounters with God in, 93–96
    reliability of, 21
Searle, John, 157
secondary causes, 36
secular humanism, 183
self-evident beliefs, 190–91
selfishness, 174–77
sensory perceptions, as veridical, 189
sensus divinitatus, 195
SESI beliefs, 191
skepticism, 91
sleep of reason, 75
slight-changes argument, 129–32
solipsism, 44, 114n16
"somewhat overlapping magisteria"
    (SOMA), 54
soul, 16–18
    in Greek philosophy, 110–11
    modern science's denial of, 15,
        106–10
    rescues libertarianism, 156
soul-body dualism, 18
soul hypothesis, 112–13
"soul-of-the-gaps" position, 107, 110,
    117, 158
spandrelists, 77, 80
special revelation, 187
SPECT camera, 86
Sperber, Dan, 67, 69
striatum, 147–48
Strong, A. H., 38
subjective probabilities, 134–35
superstition, 75
surprise argument, 132–40
survival
    and natural beliefs, 198
    in naturalistic evolution, 178–79
    only force that evolution can exert,
        172–73

Swinburne, Richard, 56, 157
synchronic determinism, 145

Taliaferro, Charles, 37–38, 126
"team spirit," 109
teleological argument, 36, 51, 55
Temple, Frederick, 38
theological anthropology, 14
theology, compatibility with science, 56
theology of nature, 56–58
Thomas Aquinas, 57
Timpe, Kevin, 156
Tooley, Michael, 130, 132, 136, 139,
    140
Torretti, Roberto, 128
true, facts as, 49
Trueblood, Elton, 101
truth, suppression of, 187
Turner, James, 35
"two realms" view (science and reli-
    gion), 47
Tylor, Edward Burnett, 113
Tyson, Neil deGrasse, 61–62

unbelief, as suppression of truth, 187

valuelessness, in evolutionary natural-
    ism, 179
van Inwagen, Peter, 55, 81
Van Til, Cornelius, 188–89
ventromedial prefontal cortex (vmPFC),
    148
visions, 96–98, 100

Warfield, B. B., 57
warrant for belief, 195
Westminster Shorter Catechism, 80
White, Andrew Dickson, 37
Wielenberg, Erik, 175–76
will to power, 172
worldview, 198–99

young-earth creationists, 39–40

Scripture Index

Genesis
book of 187
1–2 37

Leviticus
19:2 155

Joshua
10 29

Psalms
book of 188
8:5 104
19 187
19:1–4 187
96:10 . . . . .43, 44
102:25 29
104 58
104:10–15 59
121:4 59

Proverbs
5:21 73

Isaiah
6 93
6:1–5 94
7:3 94

Matthew
1–2 96
1:20 96
2:12 96
2:13 96
2:19–20 96

2:22 96
5:45 59
5:48 155
10:19 100
10:28 16
10:29 59
17:3 17
17:8 17

John
1:13 151
1:14 23
4:24 . . . . .23n2
5:17 59
6:37 151
6:44 151
8:7 167
8:9 167
15:16 151
16:8 100
16:13 100

Acts
book of 151
7:55–56 95
13:48 151

Romans
book of 186
1 186
1:18–22 187
2:14–15 170
8:16 100
9:14–18 152
9:19–24 152

11:2.................152
11:7.................152
11:29................152
14:23...............170n9

1 Corinthians
15:19...............21

2 Corinthians
5:1–8...............17
12..................95
12:1–4 95

Ephesians
1:4–5...............151
2:8–9...............170n9

Colossians
1:17...............59

1 Timothy
2:3–4..............199

Hebrews
1:3 59

James
2:26................17

1 Peter
2:8–9...............151

2 Peter
1:3 170

1 John
2:26–27............100
5 186
5:2 186
5:13................186
5:15................186
5:18................186
5:19................186
5:20................100, 186

Revelation
1 94
1:9–10 94
1:11................94
4:1–8..............95